Age Is Just a Number

Francis Brennan

Age Is Just a Number

*Make the
best of every
decade*

Gill Books

MIX
Paper | Supporting
responsible forestry
FSC® C021394

Gill Books
Hume Avenue
Park West
Dublin 12
www.gillbooks.ie

Gill Books is an imprint of M.H. Gill and Co.

978 07171 9688 3

Designed by Bartek Janczak
Typeset by Typo•glyphix, Burton-on-Trent DE14 3HE
Edited by Alison Walsh
Copyedited by Emma Dunne
Printed and bound in Lithuania by ScandBook AB
This book is typeset in 11.25 on 15.5pt, Linux Libertine.

*The paper used in this book comes from the wood pulp of
sustainably managed forests.*

A CIP catalogue record for this book is available from the
British Library.

5 4 3 2 1

Contents

Introduction   vii

1. Work and After   1
2. Your Emotional and Physical Health   27
3. Age Is an Attitude   57
4. Friendship and Relationships   81
5. Family with a Capital 'F'   103
6. Looking Good and Feeling Great   137
7. Finances for Older People   169
8. Going Home   199
9. Francis's Twenty Tips for Growing Old
   Gracefully – and with Joy!   221

Introduction

This idea came to me because I'm getting old! I never thought I'd say it, but I will be 70 this year, and although I'm still running around, I've had a couple of health scares and have begun to experience some of the losses and the challenges, as well as the benefits, of getting older. I am a diabetic and recently had a stent fitted after a heart scare, so I know what it's like when life catches up with you.

However, no matter how much giving out we do about the modern world and all its stresses and strains, there's no doubting that life for older people is a great deal better than it was even 50 years ago. For a start, our life expectancy has increased. In 1925, it was 57.4 for men and 57.9 for women; according to the most recent CSO figures, from 2016, it is 79.6 for men and 83.4 for women. That's an extraordinary leap in less than a hundred years and, health permitting, gives us an extra quarter-century in which to enjoy our lives.

We know that old age can often be a time of loss, but also of unexpected opportunity. I was happily minding my own business as a hotelier in Kerry until I was almost 60, when I was asked to do a TV show called *At Your Service*. I had no idea where it would lead, but it's been great fun, travelling all over the country meeting people. It's been all the more enjoyable because I never expected it. Life truly can be full of surprises. Yes, some of them might not be all that brilliant – but the key is to meet each change with as much positivity as we can.

There's no real 'manual' for those of us who are getting older but are still full of beans, despite life giving us a few knocks. This book will hopefully fill that gap, with lots of practical suggestions and examples from my own life and what I've learned as I've gone through it. It won't be preachy, I promise, but I hope it will have something for everyone – not just those who can afford a certain lifestyle or who have plans to travel the world, but also those looking after older loved ones, or facing health challenges, or simply wondering how to navigate the closing chapter of their lives.

My mother died in early 2020 at the ripe old age of 96, and I miss her and our daily phone calls terribly. Thankfully, she died before Covid, which I think took a lot out of all of us, particularly the elderly, as our isolation increased. But Mum was a great example of how to grow old with dignity and grace. She lived life to the full to the very last, with a constant stream of callers to the house and a full social life. I hope I grow old just like she did.

Happy reading!

From Brenn

Work and Play

There's never enough time
to do all the nothing you want.

—Bill Watterson, *Calvin and Hobbes*

I decided to start this book with something that I know I'll have to face eventually: retirement. I'm hoping to keep working for as long as possible, but I know that I'm at the gateway to the final period of my life. However as you saw in the introduction, that period might well last another 20 or 30 years. Imagine that. My poor dad died in 1988 of emphysema, he had had the disease for 17 years, and barely had time to enjoy his timid retirement, so I'm determined to make the most of the

1.

Work and After

> 'There's never enough time
> to do all the nothing you want.'
>
> Bill Waterson, *Calvin and Hobbes*

I decided to start this book with something that I know I'll have to face eventually: retirement. I'm hoping to keep working for as long as possible, but I know that I'm at the gateway to the final period of my life. However, as you saw in the introduction, that period might well last another 20 or 30 years! Imagine that. My poor dad died in 1988 of emphysema, having had the disease for 17 years, and hardly had time to enjoy his life in retirement, so I'm determined to make the most of the opportunities that I have – many of which my father gave to me – and to enjoy this phase of my life.

I was listening to the radio one day last year and the journalist Tommie Gorman was being interviewed about his retirement. What was plain to me was how much he missed the cut and thrust of the newsroom in RTÉ. 'Work keeps me alive,' he said. That's a statement I agree with. For me, work is such a large part of who I am. It gives structure to my life, provides me with lots of challenges and is very fulfilling. I consider myself a lucky man. But another thing he said interested me: that he felt he had a moral obligation to let the next generation have its time. I had never really thought of it in that way, but he's right. The next generation needs to learn the ropes, and sometimes that means that we older people need to hand the baton over. I do feel that older people still have a lot to offer from all of our years at work, but we can do this in other ways – in my case, it'd be talking in catering colleges and training up new recruits to the hotel business, passing on the skills they'll need to succeed, but leaving the day-to-day running of the Park Hotel Kenmare to others.

I'm well aware that for some of us, who are lucky enough to do work that we love, retirement is not something we relish, but others can't wait to get out the door and onto the golf course or to pursue other interests. I had a coffee with a friend the other week, and she was telling me about her retirement, and I found what she had to say very interesting. She had decided to pay her mortgage off as early as she could, so that she'd 'buy' an extra couple of years (though bear in mind that you might face penalties if you do have the extra cash to pay off your mortgage early), and then she'd made a plan. And the plan was to have no plan! She'd decided that, after 40 years of working, her priority was to be unscheduled and unstructured, to go where the wind took her and to do whatever she felt like doing at the time.

I can understand that impulse, but because I don't work to a particular schedule in my day job, I would actually like to have some structure in my retirement. At the same time, I became a TV 'personality' (I say that in inverted commas!) after a long career in the hotel business, so I suppose that's been an incentive to keep going for as long as I can before I retire. I still travel for the hotel trade shows, too, even though I no longer need to, simply because I enjoy getting out and about and meeting people. I still consider myself a hotelier, first and foremost. Having said that, in my second career, as I like to call it, there are opportunities that have come out of left field, so I want to make the most of them. If I do have a plan for retirement, it's to spend more time with friends and family, with my nieces and nephews, and to garden more. Otherwise, I'm perfectly happy to keep on working.

No two retirees are alike. Some, finances permitting, will want to travel, others will want to spend time in the garden, some will want to spend more time with family, others will want to mark things off their bucket lists, and so on. A friend of mine is returning to college to do a degree in environmental science with a view to undertaking his own rewilding project, having worked in the media for his entire life. It just goes to show that we can have second acts – and that these can be as fulfilling and exciting as our first.

Planning Principles

1. I think it pays to have a general plan, even if, like my friend, it's to have no plan. That requires planning in itself – to take up an invitation to visit a friend, to go to the movies once a week, to buy the book-club book (you can always order it from the library, just so you know!) or to indulge in the occasional treat or few days away. That way, you'll be able to factor it into your thinking about retirement.

2. Don't be afraid to ask about your entitlements. There is no need to be embarrassed about it – why would you be, when you have worked hard for your entire life, whether outside the home or not? You might be surprised what you're entitled to.

3. Think about whether you want to 'work' after your official retirement. This might be part-time, on a consultancy basis or as a volunteer, giving back to your community. Many people, myself included, find that having meaningful outside interests helps with the transition from employment to retirement. See above!

4. What hobbies would you like to explore? Have you always wanted to learn Spanish or, as in the case of a 70-year-old man I read about in the paper recently, learn to ride a motorbike? Time is the one thing you'll have at your disposal, so having some ideas about how you'd like to spend it will be just the ticket. Remember, hobbies don't have to be expensive. You can visit galleries and libraries, you can join community book groups and voluntary organisations, all of which cost nothing.

5. If you wanted to, could you make money from your hobby? Side hustles are all the rage nowadays! A friend of mine told me about an acquaintance who is a passionate fly fisherman, but his day job was in the public sector. However, someone approached him by chance and asked if he'd be interested in being a rep for a popular fishing brand. It wasn't a full-time job, but it was a sideline, and out of that grew a thriving business. The key is, he did this gradually: he built his website, mailing list and the informative videos he posts on all matters fishing

while he was phasing out his day job, so when he was ready to retire, he had a nice little earner to support him.

6. Friends are essential in life, and particularly in retirement, but ironically we can lose touch with friends with our busy lives and then find ourselves isolated when we are no longer working. Maintain your friendships now, and make sure that you have friends outside of the office and in the younger generation to keep you up to date.

7. Get to grips with technology. I say this as a man who isn't that brilliant with tech, but it's essential for us older folk. The other day, my nephew introduced me to Revolut, for example, and I was astonished that it was so easy – and so quick – to spend my money! Seriously, the younger generation are your friends here, and my nephew was a great help in showing me how to use the online banking app, how to use a virtual card and so on. We need to be aware of security issues, without getting too excited about it, and here our banks can help with security questions. Many of them have specialists in the area who will talk to you about how best to protect your account. Generation Tech – www.generationtech.ie – is a group that offers support to older people with all matters technical, which is an excellent idea. Their website has lots of information and they even have a hotline, manned

by volunteers, so if you don't have handy young-sters in your lives, give them a try. I did read somewhere about an old lady who referred to the 'Plus' channels on her TV – ITV 1 +1, RTÉ 1 +1 and so on – as 'the aftermath', which made me laugh out loud. I know what she means!

8. Plan to be a joiner – no, not someone who saws bits of wood! If work is your main source of a social life, diversify a bit. Join a community group, a sports centre, a sailing club, a group of hardy outdoor swimmers. Whatever form it takes, being part of something is essential to our well-being. I'm not a huge hobbyist, apart from my love of gardening, but I am a member of lots of hotel- and tourism-related groups and I love going to all the board meetings, as well as meeting all kinds of people on my travels.

– The Passage of Time –

It seems that as we get older time speeds up – at least, our perception of it does. As I found out in a Harvard University paper, the reason time seems to speed by has to do with the ability of our brains to process images. When we're young, we can capture so many more in a minute, or an hour or a day, than we can when we're older, so a day can seem to last for ever.

When we're old, our ability to do this declines. So time isn't actually going faster, it's just us!

However, one thing that does take some getting used to in retirement is having all those hours to fill that were once occupied by work. Some of you might even be wondering if all the years slaving away were worth it. Maybe we have regrets about roads not taken, careers we might have had or choices we did or didn't make. This is perfectly normal. If it helps, reassure yourself that you were doing what you had to do to support your family or to keep a roof over your head and pay the bills. And you succeeded! And, hopefully, you'll have got something out of your work above and beyond that – just like my father, who worked every day of his life in his shop and loved it. Whatever your situation at this stage, you'll probably have learned that life often doesn't take the shape that we expect, and all we can do is make the best of now. We simply don't know what lies around the corner.

But while we are still – hopefully – relatively healthy, it's a good idea to give some thought to how those eight or so hours a day will be filled when we retire. After the hubbub of the retirement do, there will come a time when it'll hit you – that you are now, officially, retired.

It might be a bit scary to imagine that first day post-work. Maybe you will feel relieved and delighted that you have the time to do things you enjoy. Perhaps you'll feel lonely after all the years of company in the workplace, where you felt that you were an essential part of the team. You might feel that you still have essential skills that you'd love to share. Mixed emotions are part and parcel of any life transition, whether it be having a family, moving home, a sudden illness and so on. But giving it some thought before you retire and exploring the possibilities for filling your time will make the transition easier. For example, thinking about the aforementioned career choices: would you like to try something new in retirement? Something you've always wanted to do but told yourself you never had the time to pursue?

Of course, things like being as fast as Usain Bolt or filling Elon Musk's space shuttle might be a bit far-fetched, but if you've always wanted to run, try a Couch to 5k. I've seen them all running around like mad things in Kenmare doing the Parkrun as well on Saturday mornings, and the brilliant thing is you get lots of encouragement and meet like-minded mad people! If you've always wanted to be a journalist, could you write pieces about your area of interest or hobby? There's nothing better than the internet for promoting and discussing this kind of thing. You can be as 'niche' as you like and still find an audience. So, if you have a passion for fly-tying or volleyball, why not share it? You could even have your own website and blog.

You could also practise being retired, if that makes sense. Rather than walking out the door on that last day in work, see if you can phase yourself out of work by going part-time or freelance (pension permitting) to see how the looser structure suits you. Don't panic if it seems a bit much at first – it'll get easier. Anything that allows you to get a picture of what retirement might look like will be helpful.

– Double Trouble or Singledom –

Some people envy the fact that I'm a single person: they often say things like, 'Oh, you must be only delighted to get up and go whenever you like.' Or, 'Isn't it great not to have any responsibilities in life?' I don't get too upset about it, because my choices are my own and I'm happy with them, but I've found that I've had to give my old age some thought because of my status. I don't want to assume that my family will look after me, because they have their own lives, but I also know that I might need help at some point in the future and that I have to plan for that.

According to the latest available data from the CSO, 'The share of the population aged 15 and over who were single increased from 41.1 per cent in 1996 to 43.1 per cent in 2006, but has fallen back to 41.1 per cent (1,544,862 people) in 2016.' Interestingly, however, the proportion of single populations has grown in cities such as Dublin, at 53.2 per cent, and Galway, at 53.3 per cent. That's a lot of single people, so I know that I'm not alone.

We single people used to be considered outliers, referred to as 'spinsters' or 'bachelors' – remember the term 'maiden aunt' for an unmarried aunt, or worse, 'old maid'? Apparently, the term 'bachelor' originated in the works of Chaucer, whose 'lively bachelor' spent his time carousing and jousting and generally having the time of his life! According to a fascinating article I came across in *Smithsonian* magazine, spinsters were simply women who spun yarn for a living. It was only in the nineteenth century that the term became a negative one, with writers like Jane Austen fully understanding the implications for women of remaining single. I enjoyed this description of Jane's acceptance of a marriage proposal from a Mr Bigg-Withers, which I came across on her fan website www.janeausten.org. 'Sensing the practical measure of both their situations, Jane agrees to the marriage. Bigg-Withers is due to inherit a sizeable amount of real estate and is well off. His one negative seems to be Jane's indifference to the man as a whole.' Well, that would certainly do it! She wrote to him the following day and rejected the offer, but this was most unusual at a time when women depended on men for their financial well-being.

Of course, we know all about the bachelor farmer from our own history. A newspaper article from 1914 notes that, while English bachelors amounted to 12 per cent of the population, the number in Ireland was a considerable 27.3 per cent. Farming was to blame, according to many, with eldest sons being kept on the farm to help out and thus remaining single. The implication was that you'd somehow failed at something, but now singledom is increasingly regarded as a life choice, both for men and women. This means, of course, that we will, in all likelihood, remain so into old age.

One of the biggest things single people worry about is financial security in their old age. There's no doubting that we have to give this some thought, because we'll be entirely self-reliant and unable to lean on our other halves in old age. If you can, put in place some plans as early as possible – you'll see more about pensions below and in Chapter 7. Have a think about your will and whom you'd like to leave your worldly goods to. This is particularly relevant to single people who may want to choose a particular relative or relatives to benefit from their will, rather than, say, a brother or sister. I'm just giving examples here, not suggestions!

The other thing I've had to think carefully about is EPA or Enduring Power of Attorney. I look at this in Chapter 7 also, but I've given the matter a lot of thought, because I know that the person I appoint will be responsible for my financial affairs and my medical choices in the event that I'm no longer able to do so. It's quite a responsibility. So, recently, I decided to bite the bullet and go to my solicitor to get it done. However, I was slightly miffed that I had to answer a range of questions to prove that I was mentally competent, like 'Who is the President of Ireland?' and 'What date is it today?' I got the second one wrong!

However, us singletons aren't the only people who will need to think about how life will change once we've retired. Couples may have different issues, but they still have some thinking to do. Now – i.e. *before* you retire – is the time to have that conversation! Do you have a retirement project that you'd both enjoy, like travelling together or even building your own downsized home? How much time will you spend with each other? Will you both want to be involved with the grandchildren? You might be surprised at each other's answers.

If you've been at home, the idea of your other half being under your feet all day might be disconcerting, so take a week or two of a staycation to see how you both get along. How will you divide the household tasks now that there are two of you at home? Would you like to have dinner together every evening or just once a week? I can imagine that all these things would be difficult. As a single man, I can do exactly what I like when I like, so I realise that compromise can be challenging.

Accord, the Catholic marriage care service, has some very good advice on their website, www.accord.ie. They acknowledge that while having all this time to spend together can be wonderful, it can also be stressful. A friend of mine told me about her husband getting a ladder out and climbing on the roof of their two-storey home on his first day of retirement. When she asked him what he was doing, he told her he was looking for loose slates ... She wondered if this was going to be a regular thing, but after a while, he settled down happily to pursue his own interests and gave her the space she'd always enjoyed. Another friend of mine found that her husband wanted to accompany her to her social activities, which she resented, because she felt that he should find some of his own. Sound familiar to those of you who haven't spent a lot of time together until retirement? Good to know that these issues are also entirely normal. If you are struggling to adapt, there's a lot to be said about having a neutral 'space' like a marriage counselling service in which to air any issues. No judgement is implied: you are simply working out how to navigate this next stage as a couple.

– Seeing the World –

One of the things you might like to do, either as a single person or a couple, is to travel in your retirement. But travel isn't cheap, as we know. Still, there are options for those of you who would like a little adventure in your lives, but don't want it to cost the earth.

- Have you considered house-swapping? There are websites devoted to this way of exchanging your accommodation with that of someone living in your desired location. Yes, you might have to tidy up a bit, but the bonus is the place is free! And people often swap cars, too, so transport mightn't be an issue.
- Another possibility for older folk is house- or pet-sitting. In exchange for bringing someone's dog on walkies and feeding them twice a day, you can stay in some pretty nice places. Do check that you can meet their expectations, of course. I loved the listing on one website requiring a house-sitter for six parrots! In six separate cages ... But for animal lovers, this can be a brilliant, cost-effective way of seeing the world.
- Walks like the Camino de Santiago are full of older people, who have often ventured on their own. The bonus is that you can meet up with people and just

as easily 'lose' them if you find them a bit dull! You can stay in the famous communal albergues or opt for small hotels if the thought of snoring/bedbugs doesn't appeal.

- Small group tours can be a great way of seeing the world if you're single. You won't be alone – there will be plenty of others in your situation and you will meet people with a similar sense of adventure. If you would like to go on a cruise, but can't stretch to the cost of a cabin just for yourself, you can opt to share one for half the price. I know this requires you to share with a stranger, but it also makes a cruise affordable. You never know, you might make a friend for life! Or not ... see below!

- Volunteering can be another way to see the world, while imparting some of your skills and life experience to others. Make sure that the company is reputable and that it offers real opportunities to inform and to learn.

- The cost of travel insurance can be eye-watering for older people, but do make sure to buy it. If you fall down the Spanish Steps or are suddenly taken ill, you'll be glad that you did. Check the small print carefully to make sure that it covers you for all eventualities, particularly if you have a pre-existing condition. Don't be tempted not to declare it, because it could affect your cover. A friend of mine who was being treated for cancer declared it, and while she found the extra form-filling irritating, she got exactly the cover she needed. To save money, try looking at multi-trip policies, which will cover you for a number of holidays in one year.

Talking about travelling with others reminds me of one of my favourite stories. I've always travelled with a group of friends whom I met as part of Skål, a professional organisation for people in the tourist business. When we started travelling together, there were about 20 of us, and we all had a great time together. As a group, we really gelled, and everyone was very relaxed. We never made a fuss out of paying for things, just took turns, and because I was a non-drinker, the group would buy me dinner at the end of the holiday. Perfect!

I like to do the organising because it suits me to be in charge! The only problem is that sometimes the others think that I'm in charge of everything. I have to remind myself always to expect the unexpected. People can get sick on holiday, or have a fall or get lost – all of which has happened in our little group, so I've learned to be alert for every eventuality. Once, we were in Venice and I'd organised a private tour of the crypt that lies under St Mark's Basilica. It's a part of Venice that visitors rarely see, but it once held the relics of St Mark himself and, while it might not be on the scale of the catacombs in Rome, it's very atmospheric. It's dark, winding and as sinister as you'd imagine, and it's very easy to get lost in one of its many gloomy corridors.

So, I was on extra-high alert to keep my flock together as we followed the tour guide down from the magnificent church into the crypt, listening to her tell us all about the history of the place and how many times it had been flooded over the years. As it happened, one of us had newly been diagnosed with diabetes, but was forever forgetting to bring some sugar to revive himself if he got 'low'. He wasn't used to the regime yet, so sometimes he'd give us an awful fright by fainting and needing to be revived with a sugary drink.

I'm sure you can imagine what happened next. We were in the depths of the crypt, having wandered down endless passageways, when our friend began to look a bit peaky. 'Have you any orange juice or a fizzy drink?' I asked him. He shook his head and I had a sudden vision of him needing to be stretchered out of the crypt. How on earth would paramedics even get a stretcher down here, I thought, beginning to panic.

None of us had anything suitable, wouldn't you know. 'I know,' I said, 'I'll run upstairs to the shop and get something.' I had no idea where I was or how long it would take, but I headed off, running up and down corridors like a headless chicken until I finally managed to locate the steps back up to the basilica. I hared through the church, hoping that God would forgive me, until I got to the tourist shop on the corner and ran inside. I prayed that they'd have some orange juice among the basilica key rings and models of St Mark's! Of course, there was a queue and I had to use my three words of Italian to jump to the front, miming the act of my friend fainting and explaining that I needed something sugary – and quick. I can only imagine what the lady behind the counter thought of my pronunciation of 'succo d'arancia'! I only had a €50 note, which didn't help my case, but after much grumbling the woman produced a bottle of orange juice and my change. Thanking her profusely, I ran off back down the stairs and into the crypt, racing through winding corridors and heading into dead ends and having to reverse. By the time I found the group, I had broken out in a sweat and my heart was racing. I was in a complete panic.

And there was my friend, sitting up, chatting away as if nothing had happened! Someone else had spotted him and, recognising that he was having a low-blood-sugar episode, had given him a sugary drink. There wasn't a bother on him! I drank the juice myself and swore that I'd leave them to organise themselves the next time ...

– The Nuts and Bolts –

Whether you are waiting for the moment you turn 65 or dreading it, you will still need to think about how it's going to work in practical terms. That begins with your retirement age. In Ireland, believe it or not, there is no mandatory retirement age. You'll qualify for the state pension at 66, if you have made enough PRSI contributions, but your contract of employment might state your retirement at 65 or, as in the case of a friend of mine, 60! Heaven forfend! This, in itself, raises another possibility – that we might not get to choose our retirement date. I don't want to be a harbinger of doom, but it's wise, in today's changing world, to be as prepared as you can be: for redundancy, for example, or for a situation in which you might need to avail of early retirement through illness.

The subject of pensions is enough to make my head melt, and I'll go into it in more detail – you'll be glad to know! – in Chapter 7, but the situation in Ireland is now changing. Long gone are the days when we could rely on a large pension pot in our retirement, and nowadays, with more and more people moving from job to job, many of us don't have any pension provision in place. So, as a society, we've had to think about how we help people to manage their retirement finances.

In terms of your state pension, you'll now be given the option to work until you are 70 in order to receive a higher pension. That strikes me as being a good idea, as so many of us are living longer, and it'll suit those of us who want to continue working and who are physically and mentally able to do so. I am also pleased to see that people who have done the essential work of caring for their loved ones will receive a pension too, which is only right and proper. I won't bore you with the labyrinthine way in which state pension contributions are calculated, but, according to Minister for Social Protection Heather Humphreys, we'll be able to access our PRSI records every year to see how we stand, so don't forget to do so. Alternatively, your local Citizens Information centre or Intreo centre (once the social welfare office) will be able to help you – www.gov.ie has a full list of Intreo centres, and https://centres.citizensinformation.ie/ will tell you where your nearest information centre is.

Your employer might well have provided you with an *occupational* pension scheme, even though, legally, they aren't obliged to (they are obliged to provide access to a PRSA, however, which is a Personal Retirement Savings Account). You normally take a PRSA out with a private pension provider, which will tell you at what age you can draw down your pension and how much of it you can take as a lump sum, and so on. I have one of those because during the 2008 recession I more or less lost everything else. I'm not saying this to complain, but simply as fact. I feel lucky to have anything at all, to be honest.

If you are extremely lucky, you'll have a *defined benefit* pension scheme, which basically means that you will benefit from a defined portion of your salary when you retire, but a *defined contribution* scheme means that you'll have a pension pot at the end based on the contributions you've made. Either way, if you are reading this book in your 30s or 40s, do try to plan ahead as much as you can. But, and this is a big but, do your research on pensions and savings and be prepared for a changing landscape.

This particularly applies to women. The reason I say this, before you accuse me of sexism, is because women's lives have traditionally been more of a mixed bag when it comes to working. Women may have taken time out to raise a family before returning to the workforce, as my own mother did after Dad died, or may have worked part-time for a while. It's also a fact that women tend to end up in in lower-paid, less secure employment, which can lead to gaps as far as pension contributions are concerned – and let's be honest about the pay gap that exists between men and women doing the same jobs! Ever heard of the Gender Pay Gap Information Act 2021? This requires all organisations with more than 250 employees to report any disparity between the pay of their male and female employees. According to the HR organi-sation CIPD, this stands at 14 per cent. Not something to be proud of ...

If you doubt me, the Retirement Planning Council of Ireland has a very informative piece on women and retirement – www.rpc.ie/women-retirement-and-pensions/. In fact, the council has a lot of excellent information on retirement and also conducts pre-retirement courses.

I have to confess that I hadn't even realised that pre-retirement courses were a thing until I began to research this book. That's how little consideration I gave to the subject, I'm ashamed to say. Now, however, I'm quite the expert and it's given me a few ideas for planning my own retirement, whenever that comes. The aforementioned Retirement Planning Council has courses, and if you work in an organisation your employer might well bring in experts in the area to guide you. Alternatively, Citizens Information has a host of informative articles on retirement planning.

– My Retirement Plan –

In my own case, my health scares have focused my mind on what I want out of life as I age. I know that I want to be healthy and well, to see my nieces and nephews grow and have families of their own, to keep working, which is really important to me, and to keep travelling. Many of my travel companions are in their late 80s and early 90s, and I need to keep up with them! I'm a great man for lists, so I made one of all the things that I'd like to do as I get older.

Firstly, I plan to keep stretching my brain. I'm not a great man for the puzzles or Sudoku – they test my patience too much – but did you know that learning a language can stave off mental decline by as much as five years? If you don't fancy that, you could try chess or bridge – anything that gets those wheels turning and keeps your neurons firing. Also, various universities offer programmes for the older person, where you can sample modules from undergraduate courses. DCU, for example, offers modules from the geopolitics of the Middle East to organic chemistry. If you want to progress, your module will count as a credit; if not, you can simply listen in and discuss in lectures – I'd love to do that! And all you need is yourself – no qualifications needed.

You might also consider joining your local U3A group. Not sure what it is? It stands for University of the Third Age, and in Ireland it was founded by Age Action. It's self-starting, in that local groups of older people get together to continue learning, whether it be crafts, history, creative writing and so on. And you can organise for guest speakers to come along. For a list of groups, contact Age Action – www.ageaction.ie.

I plan to be open and curious about life, particularly the bits of it that puzzle me. I try not to do any of the 'children of today don't know they're born' old-man talk. The children of today are different, of course, but rather than dismissing them, have you thought about the challenges they face? Lack of job and home security in a fluid world, climate change, war, for example? Ask your nearest young person what they think about life today and be open to their answers. You might learn something! I know that I have.

I also try hard not to think that I know it all, just because I've been around a bit longer. The longer I live, the less I realise I know! It does me good to know that I am not always right about everything, just because I'm 70 years of age.

I've also promised myself that I'll focus on happiness as I get older. I know that it can be difficult for those of us who care for partners who might be ill, or who might be ill ourselves, but even if the plans you so carefully made have gone out the window, there's always something to be grateful for. A friend of mine had cancer and was finding it tough going. A doctor said to her, 'There's always someone worse off than you.' This might not sound comforting, but it's true! I try to remember that every day.

2.

Your Emotional and Physical Health

'Find ecstasy in life.
The mere sense of living is joy enough.'
Emily Dickinson

I spent Christmas 2021 with my sister, Susan, in Sligo. I had been looking forward to putting my feet up and spending time with the family after the past few, difficult years. Sligo is full of lovely walks, and I was all set to go on a few of them with Susan and the children. However, I found that I was becoming breathless after a few steps. After a trip to the GP and a referral to a consultant, I found that I needed to have a stent fitted. It's not that big a deal in terms of complexity – it simply involves them putting in a tiny little device to unblock an artery – but I got the fright of my life! To think, I could have had a heart attack at any point. Since then, I've been careful to mind myself and to prioritise my health, both physical and mental.

I had always assumed that a lot of my health came down to my genes. However, according to *Scientific American*, 'Twin studies ... suggest genetics only account for approximately 20–30 per cent of an individual's chance of surviving to age 85.' So, if your aunty Mary lived to be 100, there's no guarantee that you will! Apparently, lifestyle choices such as smoking, drinking alcohol and eating an unhealthy diet have a much greater bearing on our health, as does stress. You'll see this in my chat with Dr Mark Rowe at the end of this chapter. However, the good news is that the other 70–80 per cent of our health is up to us.

For a start, there's a lot we can do to prevent certain conditions – something I really wish I'd known before getting type 2 diabetes and a heart problem. It can help to keep your weight within a healthy range, as being overweight can lead to a number of health conditions, something I can relate to. I can remember quite clearly the dose I got while travelling in India, which led to me losing 15 pounds in weight. Perhaps the hand of God was involved there somewhere, but I kept the weight off. Now, however, I'm on medication to make sure I don't put it on again. So, if you want to give diabetes a miss, making lifestyle choices as early as you can can really help.

With our ageing population, governments all over the world have been putting their minds to, first, prevention and, second, mitigation when it comes to disease. TILDA is a longitudinal study – that is, one that follows a group of people over the longer term – of people over 50 undertaken by Trinity College Dublin, and its findings emphasise just what a challenge we have ahead of us. When the original report came out, in 2011, we learned that the older population – those over 65 – would go from 11.4 per cent in 2011 to 22.4 per cent in 2040. That's a lot of older people! What's more, 'Over the same 30-year period, the number of people aged 80 and over is projected to rise from 130,598 to 457,962 – an increase of 250 per cent.' Of course, that means that there will be more people suffering from the illnesses of old age. However, what the study also found, and something we don't think about, is just how much elderly people give to their communities and to their families. Nearly half of those surveyed provided childcare to their children, and one-third provided shopping and housekeeping support to their children. That's quite something.

When it came to quality of life, those aged 64–75 were happier than their younger counterparts, aged 50–64, and also happier than their older ones, aged 75 and over. The younger age group are stuck between ageing parents and children, which might explain their relative unhappiness, but what struck me was that, in general, 10 per cent of older adults reported 'clinically significant depressive symptoms' and a further 18 per cent reported feeling generally depressed, even if they hadn't received a diagnosis. That's a substantial problem and one that we don't really think about when it comes to older people.

But let's take a look at our physical health first. Is there anything we can do to prevent some of the obvious bugbears of ageing? According to TILDA, older men and women are prone to conditions such as hypertension and high cholesterol, while older women are more likely to suffer from osteoporosis and cataracts. Many of us suffer from more than one condition at the same time. Osteoporosis has historically been under diagnosed. A friend of mine, a woman in her late 50s, has osteoporosis in her spine, and she tells me that she wishes she'd known more about this as a potential outcome of the menopause, so that she could have taken action sooner, such as calcium supplements and vitamin D. There are also new medications on the market that will help to slow down the effects of osteoporosis – ask your GP for further information. And don't forget the benefits of weight-bearing exercise, essential for maintaining bone density: Pilates, dancing or Zumba, jogging, skipping – all of these are weight-bearing, so try to incorporate them into your daily routine.

High cholesterol is treatable with medication, and you might also like to try making a few lifestyle changes. You could reduce the amount of saturated fat in your diet – say, from meat and cheese – and increase the amount of 'good' or 'healthy' fats – the omega-3 fatty acids that come from mackerel or salmon, but also from flaxseeds. In fact, seeds overall are good for you, and pumpkin seeds in particular are delicious! All you need to do is to sprinkle a few in your morning porridge or on a salad.

Some dietitians recommend that we take fish-oil supplements to boost our reserves of omega-3 in particular, which is thought to help our brain health, along with reducing cholesterol. I take one daily and I can't say I've turned into a genius, but it must be doing me some good! The thing about omega-3 is that we have to get it from our diets or from a supplement, and here oily fish is your friend – salmon, mackerel, sardines ... But if you're vegetarian, you can also get omega-3 from walnuts and chia seeds. Omega-6 is thought to be something we consume a bit too much of, in the form of vegetable oils, so even though it can be beneficial, we do get enough of it in our diets, generally speaking.

You can also take exercise daily – and it doesn't have to be pumping iron! Again, Dr Mark Rowe has some great advice on this below. A brisk walk during your lunch-break would be ideal, or a swim after work. Another surprise to me is that whey protein, given as a supplement, can lower your cholesterol. I thought it was only for the likes of bodybuilders and gym bunnies! However, a number of studies have shown that it has benefits for non-gym fans, too. You can add a scoop of whey protein to your porridge or include it in a smoothie – but just as you would with any lifestyle change, always check with your GP first. If you are lactose intolerant, for example, whey protein is not your friend! My local health food shop also informed me that it can be a little, well, bloating, so do your research before you buy.

High blood pressure is something all of us have to be aware of, not just older folk. However, with those of us who are over 65, it's particularly important to keep an eye on it, as it can really creep up on you. When you go to your GP, they are looking at your *systolic* reading – that is when your heart is working to push the blood out – and your *diastolic* reading, when your heart is relaxed. So, a reading of 120/80 or below is normal. A reading of 140/90, for example, would be higher and you'll want to discuss it with your doctor. Untreated blood pressure can lead to stroke, heart attack and more, but before you panic, it's treatable with medication, and, if it's not severe, little lifestyle changes always help, such as eating more fruit and veg and less salt. And, despite what you might hear, it has nothing to do with your nerves! My mother always used to joke that we were giving her high blood pressure with our antics when we were children. However, the reality is that it's down to genes in many cases and to lifestyle. We can't change our genes, but, as I've learned, we can modify our lifestyles. We mightn't love it, but we'll do it!

Ashwagandha, the Latest 'Wonder' Plant

Ashwagandha is a shrub that grows in India and has been used there as part of Ayurvedic practice. It is thought to help with stress and anxiety, along with reducing inflammation and blood pressure. That's quite the claim! According to *Medical News Today*, 'In Ayurvedic medicine, ashwagandha is considered a Rasayana. This means that it helps maintain youth, both mentally and physically.' However, most studies have been carried out on mice, not humans, so its efficacy isn't really clear, although it is considered to help with anxiety. You can take a supplement, which is generally available at your local health food shop, but as with everything else, check with your doctor first. Some supplements aren't up to scratch, and if you take too large a dose you might get an upset tummy.

Many of us face challenges in life, and a trauma or shock can leave us reeling. However, in time, we will recover and feel able for life again. Depression is not like that. It's a mental condition that can make us feel that life has no colour and that it's hard to get through the day. We might feel more tired than usual, and unable to look after ourselves as well. We might even isolate ourselves from family and friends. I wonder if many of us realise that our low mood might be a result of depression, rather than the usual ailments of old age?

If you've lost a loved one, perhaps you feel like this and wonder if you are depressed, but according to St Patrick's Mental Health Services, when we are grieving, we can experience a whole range of emotions at any one time, but when we are depressed, our feelings are more of a grey monotone. If you are feeling like this, contact your GP – there is help out there and no need to suffer in silence.

You might wonder why depression is more common in older adults. Again, according to St Patrick's, many conditions, such as Parkinson's or cancer, are linked with depression. Medications, such as sleeping tablets, steroids and beta blockers can also have depression as a side effect. It won't affect everyone – so don't panic! – but if you are feeling low for more than a day or two, talk to someone. It's not a sign of weakness: it's simply a mental health condition that requires treatment. If you fell over and broke your leg, you wouldn't leave it to heal itself, so accept that sometimes your mind can need help too.

It can be helpful to practise some form of mindfulness or meditation to help with stress. Many people swear by it as a tool to reduce anxiety and to help us live in the moment. Even better, mindful ageing is a practice specifically focusing on the benefits of mindfulness for older people. The EU has actually undertaken a pilot programme, the Mindful Ageing Project, to examine how people aged 50 and over can benefit from the practice. The programme is due to finish in 2023, but if you want to find out more, look at www.mindfulageing.eu/about. Ireland is one of the countries participating in the programme, so perhaps you'll already know about it, but if not, the platform contains lots of information and tools to help you get started. Apparently, those who practise mindfulness can live for an extra seven years, so maybe it's worth looking into.

But what exactly is mindful ageing? Well, it's basically about cultivating an attitude to ageing that sees the positive as well as the negative aspects of growing old, and emphasises the importance of living in the present and being compassionate towards ourselves and others. Now, you might have heard about 'being in the moment', but if you've ever tried it, it's actually quite difficult. Our minds flit off to the many things we have to do later or the horrible email our boss sent us earlier. However, if we practise mindfulness every day, focusing on our breath as we sit comfortably and become aware of our surroundings, we can develop a much closer connection with 'now'. A friend of mine did a meditation course during lockdown and found, to her astonishment, that there was a still, calm place right at the centre of her that she'd never known existed because she'd never tuned into it. I know, it sounds too simple to be effective! But it really does help. If you want to find out more, or to complete a course in mindful ageing, many of them are being offered online. Why not explore the benefits and see if they can work for you?

Staying Connected

I wanted to write about this subject in particular, because it's something that comes up so often for us older folk and it can really affect our mental health. As we grow older, it's natural that we will lose people close to us. I thank God every day that we had Mum for so long, but I still miss her enormously. I used to look forward to our nightly phone call and, even now, find myself reaching for my phone at 10 o'clock, before reminding myself that she's no longer here.

If we have been alive for any length of time, we'll have lost friends or loved ones, but sometimes, in old age, it can feel that we are surrounded by loss. We might also be our partner's main carer, which can be stressful and lonely. Now, more than ever, it's important to reach out to friends and family. In earlier generations these emotions were never discussed, but thankfully society is a great deal more open now, so let's take advantage of that. Join a society or club that can give you a regular outlet and go, no matter how gloomy you might be feeling; look after your body by filling it with nourishing food, which can definitely make us feel better; get out for a walk or gentle exercise every day, and don't be afraid to talk to people. In my experience, people love a chat! Another thing is the power of laughter to lighten our mood, and that can easily come in the company of friends, as well as watching silly TV shows or reading funny books.

I was asking a friend about strategies for reducing social isolation, and she recommended getting a dog. I hadn't thought about that, but she finds having one invaluable, both for the faithful companionship and for the social outlet it offers. Dogs are a great conversation starter, she tells me! She also reminded me of that Nora Ephron saying that it was important to have a dog so someone in the house would be happy to see you! Give some thought as to the age and breed you'd like. If you used to have Labradors, you don't have to get one at the age of 80. You can get a smaller and more manageable breed, or a 'couch potato' like a lurcher, who are very calming, too. You might consider an older dog, as they can be difficult to rehome from shelters but might be just the ticket for you. A puppy is wonderful, but they need a lot of care and training, and they will leave no slipper untouched, so think about whether you will be up for this challenge!

If you are worried about how you'll cope in the event of a sudden illness or injury, talk to a friend about it and agree that, even if they can't look after your beloved Fido, they will help to find the dog a temporary or permanent home if necessary. Keep a note of your dog's routine and any commands you use or treats that you give, and keep it somewhere obvious as a set of instructions in case the worst happens. And, most of all, enjoy the happiness that a dog can bring you and the connection they'll bring with other doggy owners and with the world outside.

– An Interview with Dr Mark Rowe –

While I was thinking about all of the above, I came across an excellent book called *The Vitality Mark* by Dr Mark Rowe. He's a GP based in Waterford with a special interest in lifestyle medicine and has a weekly well-being podcast called *In the Doctor's Chair*, among his many achievements. He has heard and seen just about everything and has very simple recipes for maintaining our physical and mental health as we age. I decided to interview him so that you all could benefit from what he has to say. His words of wisdom really made me think about getting old in a very different and much more positive way. Here's what he had to say.

Q: Someone once told me that our genes determine our lifespan. They'll say, 'Oh, Granny Margaret lived to be 93, so, so will I.' Is that true?
A: Well, genes do play a part, but between 70 and 80 per cent of the way our cells express themselves is down to lifestyle. So, our health span is largely up for grabs.

We actually have two ages, our chronological age – none of us can change that – but we also have our biological age, which is the miles on your clock. Staying biologically younger supports your health span, your longevity and all of the things you want to do. There's no reason why we can't stay fit and healthy and active well into our late 80s and even our 90s.

Q: Is that right? How can we plan ahead, when we could be knocked down by a bus tomorrow?! Nobody knows what's going to happen in the future.

A: That's true, but there's nothing we can do about the proverbial being knocked down by a bus! It's about taking charge of what you can control. Begin with the end in mind. Say you're 60–65 now – you can ask, 'What health would I like to have when I'm older? Would I like to be able to get some winter sun? Would I like to be able to go through the airport without having to use a wheelchair? Do I still want to get out in the garden and bend down to take care of the plants? And what about my mental health? Do I want to write books in my 80s or travel the world?' Whatever your dreams are, good health is the foundation to achieving them. To grow old gracefully, the foundation stone is to have good health. It's the greatest gift there is.

Q: Well said, but how can we nurture our health?
A: I think that there are five things we can do to improve our physical and mental health. In my book, I have a diagram of the five fingers of the hand. I call it the Hand of Vitality, and it's a really simple way of thinking about vitality in your life and how it all connects. In essence, each finger represents a part of us, with the little finger representing the heart, the ring finger the body, the third finger the soul or spirit and the fourth the mind. Care, for others and for ourselves, is represented by our thumb. All of these elements are interconnected, so improving one aspect can have a

beneficial impact on others. Let's take exercise, for example. Exercise improves your physical health but it also helps your mind by improving thought processes, easing stress and boosting emotional positivity, and in a group situation it can be a great way to strengthen relationships.

Q: I have to confess that I don't like organised exercise. I'm a great man for a walk or swim, but otherwise, I'm hopeless!
A: Well, building up a sweat is fantastic, but there are other elements of exercise that are really important as we age. For example, strength training. Your muscle mass is a leading biomarker, or indicator of healthy ageing, so you've got to stay strong, because you're losing lean muscle each year, certainly after the age of 40. I've had patients into their 80s, and I've told them to get a personal trainer and get into the gym and start lifting weights. Twenty minutes of strength training three times a week is part of the 'exercise as medicine' prescription, and not only will it strengthen your muscles, it will reverse age-related muscle loss and boost your age-related mental health.

The other thing is taking some sort of exercise for balance. It's really to prevent us from falling – yoga is terrific, Pilates is good, as is practising standing on one leg.

Q: I don't think I'd be able to stand on one leg these days!

A: Well, ideally, you need to be able to balance on one leg for at least 10 seconds, so it's important to practise. A 2022 study published in the *British Journal of Sports Medicine* found that being able to successfully balance on one leg for 10 seconds predicted survival into older age among middle-aged and older individuals. Yoga or tai chi will help, and both are gentle forms of exercise. I also recommend integrative exercise, like swimming, which tones muscles and gets the heart rate going. (As an aside here, the HSE has a page on balance exercises: https://www2.hse.ie/living-well/exercise/indoor-exercises-older-people/balance-exercises/)

Q: I've been told that getting outdoors is very important for your health.

A: It is. Getting out in nature for at least two hours once a week builds our self-confidence and boosts our mood. I call exercise in nature 'exercise squared', because it compounds all the benefits. Finally, the idea of movement is very important. One of my favourite patients is 87 years of age and he's a warrior. He loves watching soccer on TV, but every time there's an ad break, he gets up and walks around, he makes a cup of green tea or he heads out into the garden for a few moments. Regular movement breaks the corrosive grip that cortisol, the stress hormone, has on us.

Q: I'm not the best sleeper. I'm a bit of a night owl. Any suggestions for how I might improve it? I understand that it gets worse in old age.
A: Levels of melatonin, the sleep hormone, certainly get lower as we get older, and men might have to get up and go to the bathroom a couple of times a night – maybe women as well – so your sleep isn't as good. But even if your sleep requirement does go down a little bit, it's important to try to prioritise it. So, no tech in the bedroom, because the blue light destroys melatonin and stops you winding down, and don't take caffeine after lunch. It has a half-life of five to six hours, which means that half of it will still be circulating in your system at bedtime. My podcast, *In the Doctor's Chair*, has some more information on sleep, along with a whole host of other subjects, such as building resilience, being compassionate to yourself, lifestyle medicine and so on. I'd also suggest that if you're not sleeping well because your mood's a bit down, get it looked at. Go and talk to your doctor.

Q: You're right. A lot of people have been telling me that they haven't felt themselves since Covid.
A: Yes. Many people are feeling lonely and disconnected, and loneliness is a huge, huge health hazard.

Loneliness can cause falls, memory loss, heart disease, stroke; it causes the blood to thicken just like cigarette smoke does. There are a whole range of studies showing that building strong, positive interpersonal relationships is essential as we get older. Mother Teresa once said, 'Loneliness is the most terrible poverty.'

Q: Any tips to break that cycle?
A: It can be difficult to take that first step. Ironically, when people are lonely, they develop this hyper-vigilance to social threat. They know they need to get out there and reconnect, but it's not easy to do it. Thankfully, there are ways to take that first step. Perhaps you have an interest like photography or outdoor swimming. Connect your interests with joining a group. If you like gardening, join a gardening club, if you like painting, whatever it is – be willing to figure out ways to take that step. Or you can think about it in another way. Instead of waiting for people to come to you, think about how you can be a better friend or neighbour. None of us can change the world, but we can change the world around us in small ways that might make a difference.

Q: That's a great idea. I'm a fan of making small changes to improve life. I also try to be grateful for what I have, rather than focusing on what's wrong all the time.

A: Being grateful is a wonderful antidote to stress, I think. Gratitude brings perspective to the past, peace to the present moment and hope for the future. You can quote me on that! What's fundamental to surviving difficult periods in life is keeping a gratitude journal – every night, open it and write down three things that went well today. It doesn't mean that you ignore problems – far from it – but it allows you to gain perspective and a more peaceful outlook when there are challenges around you. We're not denying reality or keeping our heads in the sand: we're choosing to find things to be grateful for. I like to call it 'radical acceptance' – that is, accepting the reality of how things are today, but also understanding that there is always something that we can do to improve things, even just our own understanding of our relationship with ourselves or others. The other term I like is 'realistic optimism' – understanding that there is always something that can be done and that we can be positive about. According to the *Journal of the American Medical Association*, learning more optimism reduces heart disease by about 35 per cent!

Q: That's an astonishing statistic. If I've come in to see you in your surgery, what prescription would you give me on the way out?
A: Firstly, look after the basics. Get a good check-up on your physical health to start with. A lot of

the things that can destroy your lifespan are silent: one in three people in Ireland has high blood pressure and doesn't know it. It's a silent condition. Cholesterol is the same, so get that checked. Have a DEXA scan to check your bone density. There can also be a family history of bowel or heart problems, so get that attended to. Don't ignore the obvious. Knowledge is power to take action, as they say. After that, I'd say never stop growing or learning and don't allow the mindset of other people, or your own, to determine what you can and cannot do. I've seen people start new businesses at 80, build new houses, travel the world, do a new degree – why not?

We were always told that our brain cells died off as we got older, but now we know that there's this thing called neuroplasticity, which means that we can improve our brain's flexibility throughout our life.

Q: Yes, I've heard about that! What can I do to keep my brain in good shape?
A: There's so much you can do to build new brain cells: take exercise, practise mindfulness ... The food you eat can have a massive impact on building new brain cells, as can the quality of your sleep and feeling engaged – as I say, 'flow to grow'. You're in a flow state when you're challenging yourself but aren't stressed. However, you need to join the dots. Make the connection between your intentions and

what happens. I call this the Intention Gap: you can make all the plans in the world, but the road to hell is paved with good intentions! This is where having an accountability partner is great. You can keep each other on track.

Q: That's great advice.
A: Thank you! I'd add that if you want to make small positive changes, start with *why*. Why do you want to exercise more or improve your sleep or diet? The Japanese call it *ikigai* – your purpose: for example, 'I value health'; 'I want to travel'. Connect your changes to your why. And frame it positively and realistically. For example, saying, 'I'm not eating chocolate or crisps ever again' – well, your willpower is strong on a Monday but by Thursday you're saying, 'Give me chocolate. I deserve it!' I say, rather than giving up chocolate, why not change to dark chocolate? It's one of the best foods we can eat – dark chocolate (more than 70 percent cacao) has lots of flavonoids, which feed the great flora in your microbiome and release nitrous oxide, which opens up your blood vessels. Dark chocolate is on the top shelf, along with beetroot, turmeric and all the vegetables!

Q: Which reminds me of nutrition. Do you have any suggestions for this age group in particular?

A: I'm a big fan of two things when it comes to diet.

1. Mindful eating, which is a practice that involves really paying attention to what you eat, noting hunger and fullness cues and avoiding distraction so that you really get a sense of what your food is like and, more importantly, when you've had enough.
2. The Mediterranean diet is the diet that we should all be aiming for if we want to improve our health. Studies have shown that in certain communities people's longevity can be directly connected to their diet.

Q: As I discovered when I looked into it for this book!

A: Exactly. A diet high in unsaturated fats, such as extra virgin olive oil, nuts and seeds, and that incorporates a large range of colours from fresh veg and fruit – i.e. that's largely plant based – is ideal. Fatty fish, such as tuna, salmon and sardines, are very beneficial, as are moderate amounts of dairy, such as unsweetened Greek yoghurt. Pulses are brilliant also: beans, lentils, chickpeas and so on.

Q: That could be a struggle for some Irish people. We love our meat!

A: That's true, but if we are prioritising health, we can eat small amounts of good-quality meat – the key is to add more fruit and vegetables into the mix. I much prefer a positive message, such as to include more colour and more variety in your diet, rather than saying 'you can't eat this' or 'you can't eat that'. No one likes being told what they can't have, do they? In my book, I use the case study of my patient, Brian, who had a family history of heart disease and didn't look after his diet. He, too, had a heart attack, but luckily he got to hospital on time. He was given a second chance. He didn't waste it! He really embraced the idea of mindful eating, focusing on nutrients rather than calories and eating more fruit and veg every day. Now, he's lost five inches off his waist and grows his own veg!

Q: That all sounds logical and achievable. In real life, is it that easy?
A: Making lasting change is always a challenge, but I like to put the emphasis on developing healthy eating habits and awareness rather than going on a diet. Diets may work in the short-term, but over the longer-term, positive lifestyle change is what really matters.

And on that positive note, thank you, Dr Mark Rowe. *The Vitality Mark* is published by Gill Books and available at all good bookstores. His podcast, *In the Doctor's Chair,* is easily found online @drmarkrowe, and there's more information on his website: https://drmarkrowe.com/

A Simple Breathing Exercise

1. Settle down on a firm chair with back support. Relax your shoulders and make sure that your feet touch the ground.

2. Close your eyes or focus on one spot on the wall in front of you.

3. Tune into your breathing, and notice where you can feel it most: in your nose, chest, tummy ... focus on that breath coming in and out of your body. Listen to it and become aware of your chest or tummy rising and falling in time with your breathing.

4. If your mind wanders, just bring it gently back to the breath. Continue for a further 10 minutes, just breathing, and then expanding your awareness to your surroundings: the birds in the garden, the wind, the traffic ...

5. Many people use guided meditations to help them focus and there are vast amounts of them online. The website https://www.mindfulageing.org/ contains a huge amount of information on mindfulness and an online course to complete at home.

– Crashing into Cows –

I will finish this chapter on a lighter note, having just remembered a story about crashing into a herd of cows and ending up in hospital in Tralee. It does have relevance to health, honestly! Bear with me ...

I was in the Park Hotel Kenmare at the time, sometime in the 1980s, and I'd left the hotel at 7 a.m. because I had a Blue Book meeting in Dublin – that's the guidebook to Ireland's most luxurious hotels and guesthouses. Anyway, I was driving along towards Killarney and I came around a bend, whereupon all these cows came flying out of a ditch. I applied the brakes, and of course the back of the car swung like you'd see in a Steve McQueen movie into a pile of gravel at the side of the road. I pulled back too quickly, and the car rolled over. Three times I rolled, and then the car began to skid along the road on its roof. All I could think was, *Please don't hit a cow.* That would really confuse the issue, as you can imagine.

As I slid along, all of the cows' hooves went flying by, and all I could think was, God Almighty, that's a terrible noise, as the car skidded along the road. The next thing, I noticed that I was heading for the ditch. I thought, *Don't hit a pole, because it'll knock the head off you.* Thankfully, I bypassed that and slid into the field, where I finally came to a halt, the car a mangled mess around me.

I was still conscious, but upside down in the car, hanging by my seatbelt, blood pouring out of my nose. The car was making an ominous hissing sound and

I was terrified that everything would blow up, so I said to myself, 'Get out of the car, quick.' I couldn't quite reach the catch of the seatbelt, so I sucked my tummy in and pushed my hand back and I just got it. I fell down with a thump that made my head throb, grabbed my briefcase, which had my life in it, and climbed out through the windscreen, because the doors were jammed shut.

As I was clambering out, two young fellows appeared. 'Are you all right?' they said, as they stood over me. They were two builders, on their way to work, and they'd seen the whole thing. 'Do you know you turned over three times?'

'Did I?' I said. I'd lost count! Of course, there were no mobile phones in those times, so I said, 'Will you ever go back to the garage and phone for an ambulance?' Off they went, and at the same time I spotted the local farmer, who I'd seen many times on the road before, running up towards me, pulling on his trousers. I'd clearly got him out of bed.

He rushed towards me, a concerned look on his face. 'What happened?'

I suppose the mangled car and my appearance should have told him, but I explained, 'There were cows on the road and I skidded and crashed.'

'What cows?' he said, as we both looked at the herd of cows on the road in front of us. Quick as a flash, he scooted them in off the road into the field.

Being a Kerryman, he knew that it was far better if there had never been any cows on the road, if you catch my drift!

Next thing, another man appeared, introducing himself as the farmer's brother. 'Come into the house,' he said, 'and we'll make you a cup of tea.' We all shuffled off in the direction of the house. Now, when I went into the kitchen, it was obvious that it was a house occupied by two bachelor farmers, with empty mugs and newspapers scattered around, but I was still placed in the sitting room, as an honoured guest! I had a big gash on my hand and it was pouring blood, and it started to run down my arm and drip onto the carpet. I pulled out the *Sunday Independent* and put it on the floor and let my hand drip all over it. I could hear the kettle boiling in the kitchen and then a voice said, 'Get him a cup of tea with a load of sugar!' It was their mother, who'd been bedridden for years. She'd been a nurse so knew exactly what to do. I managed to locate a hankie with my good hand and wrapped it around the gash, so I wouldn't destroy the newspaper further.

Eventually, the ambulance arrived and, thankfully, the nurse on board was able to bandage my hand with a lovely big bandage, wrapped securely around my wrist. Off we went in the ambulance, arriving at the hospital in Tralee a short time later. I was rolled into the ward and transferred to a trolley in a cubicle.

There was nobody in A&E (those were the days!), so while I waited to see the doctor in my cubicle, I could hear the nurses chatting about the weekend that had just passed. 'Did you dance with Joe?' 'I bought a lovely cake for her birthday.' 'Did he send flowers – oh, isn't that nice?' and so on! Next thing the cry went up, 'Has anyone got a scissors?'

'No, I don't,' shouted one nurse, followed by another. 'No, neither do I.' 'They took the scissors upstairs.' *The* scissors. There was only one pair in the whole hospital …

By this stage, I had a huge bump on my head, and when I put my finger in my ear, blood came out. Uh-oh, I thought, my brain is bleeding. I began to panic. 'Hello?' I said.

The curtain was pulled back and the nurse said, 'He'll be with you in a second. He was at home and is coming in right now.'

'Fine,' I said. I'd obviously got the doctor out of bed!

Next thing, the curtain opened and the doctor poked his head in. 'What's the problem?' he said, in a heavy French accent. I didn't know what he wanted me to say – I was sitting there with my hand aloft like Frankenstein, blood pouring out of my ear!

He came in, muttering to himself, and started trying to pull the bandage off, but it wouldn't come away. He turned to the nurse. 'Have you got a scissors?'

'No, doctor,' she said. 'No scissors.'

The blessed scissors! 'Excuse me,' I said. 'If you open my briefcase, I have a pair of scissors.' I'd got it in a Christmas cracker and thought it'd come in handy. How right I was!

The nurse bent over to retrieve the scissors and the doctor kept tugging at my bandage. Eventually, it pulled away and there was this huge spurt of blood that hit the ceiling of the cubicle. It hit the doctor and sprayed blood all over his shirt and he jumped back. The nurse jumped back too and dropped the briefcase, and my life was all over the floor of A&E – tablets, passport, et cetera. I was mortified – but I could see the scissors ...

'Ah, *non*,' he said, pointing to his shirt. 'Nurse, have you got a ... you know ...? I don't know the word.' He began to mime lifting something over his head and tying it behind his back. While I lay on a trolley, dying, he was doing charades, I thought.

'An apron?' I said.

'Yes, yes, an apron,' he said. 'Nurse, have you got an apron?'

In fairness, the apron appeared and he stitched my hand brilliantly – you can't see where the scar is today. I had to have an X-ray, and it turned out that the blood in my ear was a piece of glass that had gone in and cut it. There was no bleeding from the brain, thank God.

I ended up recuperating in the hotel for two weeks. Every day, I put Optrex in my eyes, morning and night, to keep them clear. When I went to the consultant three weeks later, he took one look at me and said, 'Are you sure you're Francis Brennan, the same man who was in the accident?'

'Of course it's me,' I said.

'There's no way, after you did that damage to your nose, that you could be clear of bruising under the eyes.'

'Well, I put Optrex in them, morning and night,' I explained. The Optrex had cleared the congealed blood that would have given me bruising under my eyes.

'Well,' he said, 'I never knew that.'

And that's the end of the story!

P.S. The car was a write-off, but I sold it for £400, because it had a great radio!

3.

Age Is an Attitude

'With age comes wisdom,
but sometimes age comes alone.'

Oscar Wilde

From my discussions with Dr Mark Rowe, I firmly believe the quote above from Oscar Wilde: that so much of how we deal with our old age depends on what our attitude is towards it. We can be a very old 70, moaning and groaning about our ailments and how awful being old is, or we can be a youthful 90, like the older woman I read about in the newspaper recently, who went skydiving at 93! Of course we can't control our health or circumstances, but what we can control is our perspective on ageing and our behaviour. But does a positive attitude really benefit us? I think it does, and I have the proof to show it.

I was fascinated by the experiments of Dr Ellen Langer in this area, which I read about in the *New York Times*. In the early 1980s, she transformed a hotel in New Hampshire into a 1950s time capsule, complete with furnishings, music and reading material from that era. Can't you just imagine the Buddy Holly and Elvis pictures on the walls, the linoleum flooring and the 1950s television sets? Into this environment, she introduced 8 men in their 70s, with instructions to behave as if they were 20 years younger. For example, not only were they to discuss 1950s baseball scores and read 1950s magazines, but they were also to walk up the stairs unaided and carry their own items in and out of their bedrooms. To complete the picture, nothing in their environment was to come from the 1980s, not one single photo or device.

They had been tested before the experiment, checking physical dexterity, memory and so on, and after five days in this environment, they were tested again. Their scores on several key markers were higher than they had been 5 days before and higher than a control group who had gone to the hotel without any instructions to behave as if they were 20 years younger. According to the *New York Times*, 'They were suppler, showed greater manual dexterity and sat taller – just as Langer had guessed. Perhaps most improbable, their sight improved. Independent judges said they looked younger.' Isn't that interesting? As Dr Langer said in a lecture, 'Wherever you put the mind, the body will follow.'

This became known as the 'counterclockwise experiment' and it was really ahead of its time, understanding that, while ageing is a biological process, so much of it is influenced by what's going on in our heads and the connection between mind and body. That's something I learned from Dr Mark Rowe, but I also firmly believe this and have seen it in my own life. Part of the reason my mother lived independently until her mid-90s, I believe, was because she was sociable and engaged with everyone around her, and also had great relationships with her children.

However, our attitudes have a lot to do with the prevailing culture and our society's view on ageing and the elderly. In China, for example, parents often lived with their adult children until quite recently, when so many migrated to large cities to work, leaving their elderly parents behind. The same is happening in India, where a newlywed woman generally moved in with the in-laws – again, this is changing as Indian society changes. However, what's different in these societies is that the elderly are revered, so much so that China introduced mandatory visits to parents by their children, enforceable by penalties or even imprisonment! If they introduced that here, there'd be war! The important thing is, they are not seen as a burden, something that needs to be carried or shouldered. In Japan, for example, older people are referred to using the suffix -*san*, a term of respect, and a person's 60th birthday, the threshold of old age, is considered to be a very big deal. Sixty is the new forty!

How Old Are You Mentally?

This fun quiz will give you the answer. I'm between 30 and 39, it would seem! According to the quiz-masters, this means that I'm 'still relatively fresh', like a day-old loaf of bread ...

1. **What do you like to do with your free time?**
   A: Stay in with a good book.
   B: Go out with friends to a nightclub.
   C: Dig out my herbaceous border.

2. **What is your typical bedtime?**
   A: Before 9 p.m. – I'm an early bird.
   B: After 9 p.m. – I'm an owl.
   C: Bedtime is for old people.

3. **What time do you get up?**

   A: 6 a.m., to do some tai chi and go for a run.

   B: 11 a.m. – I can't function in the morning.

   C: I never get up in daylight.

4. **What do you like most about Christmas?**

   A: Watching *It's a Wonderful Life* and *The Wizard of Oz*.

   B: Having my family around for a big dinner.

   C: The presents!

5. **Are you hip?**

   A: What's hip?

   B: No, but I'm due a knee replacement next July.

   C: Sure, I'm down with the kids.

6. **Do you like DIY?**

   A: I believe that 'Elephant's Breath' is a very popular colour at the moment.

   B: I have my paint roller and measuring tape with me at all times.

   C: God, no. I have a 'little man' to do that stuff.

7. **What kind of social media do you use?**

   A: I haven't been the same since they got rid of Yahoo.

   B: WhatsApp – the neighbourhood-watch rota is on it.

   C: TikTok – I'm a sucker for the silly-animal videos.

8. **What's your taste in music like?**

   A: You can't beat Frank Sinatra.

   B: I'm a regular at Covent Garden for the opera.

   C: German techno is your only man.

9. **What's your favourite book?**

   A: *Gone with the Wind.*

   B: Anything by Jane Austen.

   C: *American Psycho.*

10. **Your daughter buys you a new iPhone for Christmas. What do you do with it?**

    A: Swap it for a mobile phone that I can actually use, with big buttons.

    B: I still have my rotary land-line from 1973 and there's nothing wrong with it.

    C: Fill it with the latest apps and my Spotify playlist.

11. **A friend suggests a weekend away on Ibiza. How do you respond?**

    A: Great! A chance to rock my new party outfit.

    B: I believe Ibiza has a lot of ancient Greek temples on it.

    C: No thanks, I'm off on a cruise to the Bahamas.

12. **You're happily single but your friend puts your profile on a dating app. How do you respond?**

    A: I might meet some interesting people.

    B: I don't date: I prefer a good book and a nice glass of wine.

    C: Wahay – here's to some lovely free dinners!

13. **Your son asks you to mind his baby daughter for a couple of hours while he goes to the movies with his partner for the first time in six months. Do you say:**

    A: Of course! I'd be delighted – and here's some cash to buy yourselves a nice meal after.

    B: I can manage the second Friday of September 2024 and only because my walking club has been cancelled.

    C: Does she like gin? I have a cocktail party to go to.

If you answered mostly A, you're like a fine wine – ageing well. B: You could do with some improvement. C: You have the mental age of a teenager.

– Old and New Attitudes –

I'm a great fan of TED Talks, because I think you can learn such a lot in a few minutes, and about all kinds of things, from sailing to ancient history. I watched one recently given by the geographer and Pulitzer Prize winner Jared Diamond in 2013, when he was a slip of a thing at 75. As part of his job, he studied 'traditional' societies in New Guinea and found that, to them, the elderly are very important and need to be looked after by family until the day they die naturally. This is because they are a valued resource: they mind the grandchildren, make tools and pass on the kind of knowledge that this society values.

This he contrasts with the way we treat the elderly in modern societies like our own, which 'places a high value on work', and when you can't work, well, you're not useful. And because of the emphasis on 'self-reliance and independence' we look down on the dependent older person. What's more, because technology has changed our society so quickly, we don't look to older folk as repositories of knowledge, but as technophobes, who are unfamiliar with Google and the TV remote! This rings true with me, most definitely. I have no problem at all with growing older, but I know that many might consider me a bit 'past it', because I don't Google everything and download all sorts of things.

However, Diamond's goal in the talk was to find ways in which older folk can be useful to society. Firstly, those of us who are parents can be invaluable as babysitters to young children because we have the experience of raising our own families and we also – hopefully! – love our grandchildren. And, as he points out, 'They are unlikely to quit their job, because they've found another job with higher pay looking after another baby!' While you might think this only applies to those who have children and grandchildren, I know just how valuable relationships with young people can be. I am good friends with my nieces and nephews, and it really keeps me young.

Diamond also made the point that we can learn from traditional societies in making use of our elderly folk as repositories of knowledge and memory. Older people can remember terrible events like World War II, information which is still valuable to younger generations. As an example, a friend of mine told me that her son was studying the Troubles in Northern Ireland as part of his history curriculum, and she was able to give him much-needed context and detail from her own lived experience. Mind you, I was amused recently when a friend told me that he'd made a joke in an email about a colleague being as easy to find as the elusive Lord Lucan. The reply: 'Who's Lord Lucan?' Bless ... perhaps this shows why we oldies need to be kept around! On a more serious note, if we want to learn the lessons of the past, surely it makes sense to turn to people who can remember it and who can bear witness to it?

Also, as Diamond pointed out, while older people might not be great at manual dexterity or flexible thinking, they are excellent at using judgement, based on their lifetime's experience of human relations, and are generally less ego-driven, making better administrators and supervisors than young people. I'm just saying! I can see what he means. I'm much less interested nowadays in furthering my career or achieving work goals than I was when I was in my 20s. I still enjoy work, but I know that friends and family and spending time together matters more.

I found it interesting that Diamond felt we had much to learn from societies that we might consider 'primitive'. The Western world represents progress, dynamism and achievement for so many, not to mention economic opportunity. However, his point was that our society will be all the richer for welcoming and integrating older people into it: we can learn from their wisdom and self-confidence, their decades of life experience, and they can help younger generations to flourish. I think that's a great idea! I found this a fascinating talk which helped me to see ageing in a different way – do watch it.

– It's All in the Mind –

I rang a friend of mine recently, and she told me all about the sailing lesson she'd taken the previous week. Aged 60, there she was, hunched over in a boat the size of a bathtub, capsizing all over the place! She didn't mind a bit, because she felt that she was really learning something new. She was challenging herself to learn a skill, one that was completely unfamiliar to her. At the end of the lesson, she told me, she felt exhausted but totally alert.

Learning a new skill can really keep our brains flexible as we age. According to the *Scientific American*, it's not good enough to simply *maintain* our mental agility as we age, something we are all encouraged to do: it's the *growing* that counts. If you'll remember, Dr Mark Rowe talked about neuroplasticity, which is our brain's ability to change and adjust, growing new neurons when we learn things. (It can also change and adapt if we have a brain injury.) So, while it's great to do our crossword puzzles and the knitting we've always enjoyed, it's actually important to learn new things as well. And, ideally, more than one new thing. A study in the *Journal of Gerontology* found that a group of adults had improved cognitive skills and memory function after three months of learning three different skills at the same time: Spanish, drawing and using an iPad. Before you panic, they just wanted to prove their hypothesis that older folk could learn like young children, who are learning a variety of new skills every day in school. And they can! According to the researchers, 'focusing on growth rather than maintenance allows the learner to make mistakes and fail in the short-term, while improving in the long-term'.

And that's the key, I think. How many of us are afraid to learn something new because we worry that we'll be no good at it? That we'll somehow 'fail'? Well, the good news is that, while it might take us a little longer to get the hang of things at a certain age, we can really benefit from it over the longer term. Just because society might think that old dogs can't learn new tricks doesn't mean that we have to agree with it!

According to *Harvard Health*, the newsletter of Harvard Medical School, we can do a few things to keep the wheels turning. Learning a new language or skill, such as a musical instrument, is important, but your work can keep you sharp also, as can volunteering or mentoring a young person. A positive attitude is also essential, they say. No talking about 'senior moments' or saying, 'I can't remember anything', because that can actually contribute to memory issues. Instead, they suggest, remind yourself how good your memory still is, in spite of everything you have to remember!

Are you someone who is always looking for their keys or phone? Don't get too het up about it, they say. Instead, prioritise tasks that really matter and use beeping key fobs, calendar reminders and mobile phone messages to remind yourself of the less-important stuff. And if you want to remember somebody's name, which always gets me, repeat it when you're introduced to them. 'So, Mary, where did you go to school?' That way, you'll remember it! Clever and easy. And the really important thing that's worth repeating: according to *Harvard Health*, memory loss is not actually a function of old age, but might have more to do with neurological issues, so there you go!

Having said that, this quote on memory from journalist Tim Dowling made me laugh:

'Being old means having to contend with the enormous, invisible volume of everything you have done and completely forgotten about. At the age of 20 you've lived so little you can remember virtually all of it; by the age of 60 you will have forgotten entire holidays, scores of books you've read, hundreds of arguments, upwards of a thousand former acquaintances, all the popular music released between 1999 and 2004 and at least ten Netflix passwords.'

The Recipe for a Long Life

There's a famous article in *National Geographic*, 'The Secrets of Long Life' by Dan Buettner, that identified places in the world where people were living longer and better and took a guess at why. Buettner called these places 'Blue Zones'. Any guesses where? Okinawa, Japan was one. Sardinia, Italy was another, and then California. And while the reasons for longevity varied, what they all had in common were the following:

- Regular exercise
- Connection with family
- Eating lots of fresh fruit and veg
- No smoking

If you notice, the only 'don't' on this list is 'don't smoke' – the Sardinians enjoyed a glass of red wine daily, for example. The others are all 'dos'. And while we might not be able to milk four cows and walk the mountains of Sardinia like the men in the longevity study, we can learn something: activity keeps us young. Interestingly, Sardinian women did not live as long as their men, and it was surmised that this was because they took on the stresses of managing family finances and other worries. So, share out the burdens seems to be the message here – step up, gentlemen!

Another thing that struck me was the importance of spirituality to older people in the article. An elderly woman from Okinawa pointed to this as one of the reasons for her longevity, and the study also found that Seventh Day Adventists in California managed to live to 100! I find that my faith gives me great comfort, but I completely respect those for whom organised religion doesn't have the same meaning. To me, faith has been a source of comfort and a feeling that I'm not alone in the world. I also love the sense of camaraderie that comes with meeting people and chatting to them after Mass. When I'm in San Francisco, for example, I always go to a lovely church in Chinatown for Mass, and, every single time, I'm invited back to someone's house for coffee.

Like everyone else, my faith has been tested. When my brother John was diagnosed with non-Hodgkin lymphoma, I prayed for his recovery every day. He did recover, but the disease never goes away and it has needed to be treated again. I really admire the way John has focused on getting better each time with equal determination, then just getting on with life. My faith helped me to deal with it, but every one of us has our own beliefs and we deal with challenges in different ways. I just know what works for me.

I go to Lourdes every year with the Kerry Diocesan Pilgrimage, and I always look forward to it. Like so many things, Covid interrupted our travels, but it looks as if we'll get the show on the road again in 2023. In spite of all the crowds and the souvenir shops, Lourdes is a very special place for so many people. I'm always struck by people's belief and faith that God will grant them a cure for themselves or for their relative. I can still remember one occasion when I had only just started going there and I was helping out at the baths. These are huge stone baths in which the pilgrims immerse themselves fully, just as Bernadette was told to by Mary, and our job was to help disabled people to be lowered into the water. This German man had come along with his son, who was severely disabled, and he was desperate for a cure, because, as he told me, 'Who will mind my son when I'm gone?' The son wasn't cured, and, to be honest, I didn't fully understand why God saw fit to make others well but not him. I had to accept that that was the case, but I was never able to return to the baths again, because the experience had been so emotional. Instead, I helped out in the kitchen, and for some reason I didn't stop believing. When we pass someone in the street, we never really know what they are going through, do we?

But 'spirituality' doesn't have to mean 'religion'. It can simply mean connecting with something greater than ourselves, whether this is nature or God, whatever he or she means to you. Or, like the Seventh Day Adventists, following a diet rich in fruit and veg and shunning alcohol and smoking – I'm just putting it out there! Also, the Seventh Day Adventists rest on their Sabbath, which is a Saturday. Maybe there is something to taking a break, whether we observe a religion or not?

A sense of purpose also seems to be essential to growing old gracefully – a feeling that you can still contribute in a positive way to the lives of others. Many people do this through volunteering, such as my friend who teaches English to people new to Ireland. She loves meeting people from all over the world and listening to their experiences, and she feels that it really takes her out of herself. I like to stay involved with the tourism industry and – hopefully – share my skills and experience. What do you think you could offer? Maybe you're a demon bookkeeper, or you would like to spend an hour a week mentoring a young person? Maybe you'd like to help a child with reading or music? If so, have a look at Volunteer Ireland – www.volunteer.ie – to see what might suit you in your area.

– I Regret Nothing ... –

It's tempting, when we get old, to spend time looking back over our lives and asking ourselves if we've done a good job with what we've been given. We might think about roads not taken, opportunities missed, friendships that we let drift. Sometimes, with the finishing line in sight, we can become bogged down in regret. It's impossible to live without having some regrets about bad decisions or chances not taken, but I think that these can really shape our attitude to growing old. We can be very hard on ourselves and wish that we'd done better instead of celebrating all of the things that we did well. It's perfectly normal to have regrets – they are what make us human, as this little story from my own life illustrates.

When I was younger, I always wanted to go to America. That was where the excitement was, and, because it was home to so many famous hotel groups, to me, it was also the land of opportunity. And so, one day in 1978, when I was working in Parknasilla Hotel, a man by the name of Edwards came to stay. I was terribly excited, because he was head honcho of Hilton Hotels, and there was no way I was going to miss the opportunity to meet him. I thought to myself, *He's Mr America and I need to have a chat with him*, which I duly did before he left. He was very kind to me, and he said, 'Here's my card. Send me your CV and we'll take it from there.' Now, this would all be conducted via snail mail, because there was no email or WhatsApp in those days, so it all took place over the course of months, if you can imagine that!

I got my CV together and wrote him a letter, and a few weeks later I got his reply, telling me that a Mr Benny Martin, food and beverage manager of the

Hilton Hotel group in Chicago, would be in touch. Sure enough, a letter arrived not long after from Benny. The first thing he said was, 'Would you by any chance be a son of Maura Brennan?' I had no idea where that was coming from, until I went to see Mum in Sligo a couple of weeks later. 'Oh yes, he took me on the bar of his bicycle to a dance in Ballintubber in 1940,' she told me! He had also begun his working life in Jurys Hotel in Sligo. My confirmation that I was indeed Maura Brennan's son sealed the deal. Benny Martin informed me via letter that they'd be applying for a green card for me to work in the States and would be in touch. I was on cloud nine, as you can imagine.

Then, lo and behold, we had a postal strike that year and it went on for six months. Not a letter or a postcard or a bill did we receive at Parknasilla. What's more, the telephone-connection system was out of service too, so there were no phone calls either. At the end of it, sometime in May, we got a mountain of letters at the hotel, including one from the US Embassy in Dublin to say that I was to appear on 11 February to make the case for my application for a green card. I thought that, given the strike, they'd give me some leeway, so I rang the American Embassy and they said, 'No, you either come on 11 February or not at all.' The Americans didn't make allowances for postal strikes. I never did get to America at that time. Do I regret it? I was disappointed at the time, but now I realise that my life has been a thousand times better here in Ireland. Maybe I would have done well in Hilton Hotels, but even if the hotel business in the US is glamorous, it's a high-pressure environment. Kenmare is exactly where I was meant to be.

So, how can we stop regrets from overtaking us as we age?

- I think the first thing we need to do is forgive ourselves. We did our best at the time and made our decisions based on what we knew then. Beating ourselves up about it now won't change things.
- If you find regret filling your mind, talk it through with somebody – a trusted friend or somebody neutral. You might find that it doesn't sound quite as bad as you'd feared.
- Don't hang onto resentments from the past. They can be very self-defeating at our age, when perhaps there's not a lot we can do about them. Try to let them go.
- Learn from your mistakes. If you've made a bad decision, think about what it's taught you, then take this knowledge forward to your next decision. Don't be afraid to make decisions either – not making a decision is a form of decision-making, when you think about it!
- If you feel that you haven't been as successful as you'd hoped, ask yourself, 'Is this really true?'

Perhaps you didn't get the job of your dreams, but you raised a family or had a happy marriage. Perhaps, like me, you remained single, but focused your energies on your work – what's wrong with that? Everyone is different and we should celebrate that.

- Look at your younger self with compassion. If you were a bit foolish, well, isn't that normal and natural? When I first sat the Leaving Cert, for example, I made a hash of it, but when I knew what I wanted to do, I was able to tackle it again and get what I needed to start my career in hospitality. I could look back and think that I was an awful eejit, but I was only 17 – and what 17-year-old isn't an awful eejit!

- 'Try again. Fail again. Fail better.' Samuel Beckett famously said this about failure. He's right. Failure can feel painful, humiliating even, but imagine if we'd never even tried? Now, there's something we'd regret!

- Connect with loved ones – they'll give you much-needed perspective and support.

- Live in the moment. The past is gone, the future is yet to be, so now is really what matters. Connecting with nature can be great to keep us grounded. I love getting out in my garden to be mindful. A friend of mine loves going for a sea swim. Another loves meditation. Whatever gets you in the 'now' is terrific.

- Be part of the outside world and enjoy it. Just because you're not working any more doesn't mean that you have to stay at home for ever. Find a book club, join a museum or gallery friends group, attend lectures at a university (there are schemes which facilitate this). And if you live in the country? There's no doubt that socialising can be harder, but it's still there. Active Retirement Ireland will have details of groups in your area, or the Irish Men's Sheds Association might interest you. www.seniorcare.ie has a listing of various organisations. Fáilte Isteach is a new scheme where older people can volunteer to help new arrivals in Ireland with English language skills. But if you're feeling lonely, don't suffer in silence. Seniorline is a confidential phone service for older people in need of a chat. It can really help to have a sympathetic ear. https://www.thirdageireland.ie/seniorline.

So, as you can see, being old needn't mean that we have to retire to the living room and snooze beside the fire, that we have to 'stay in our lane' and just be old and be quiet about it. Because we are living for so much longer, it's more important than ever that we find a way to live that makes the very most of our time, our values and our skills.

The Lighter Side of Senior Moments

I came across a thread recently – that's an internet conversation, for us oldies – in which various people were discussing the amusing things their older relatives said. I did love them, such as the older woman who told her nephew that another relative had bought a new house: 'And it has a lovely conservative on the back.' Then there was the woman whose mother always ordered a 'Cinzano' when they went out for coffee. She meant 'cappuccino'! Not to mention the lady who told her son that a neighbour had bought a new car: 'It's one of those Ford Fiascos.' And those are the printable ones ... I'm sure you have your own.

4.

Friendship and Relationships

'What though youth gave love and roses,
age still leaves us friends and wine.'

Thomas Moore

I'll begin this chapter by telling you about my
schoolfriend Frank. I know he'll be mortified, but
as we've shared so many years of friendship, he'll
forgive me! We met as schoolboys, and we've hol-
idayed together many times over the years. We're
opposites, but maybe that's why we get on so well. I
like to think that he's an old grump and that I never
complain! After many years of friendship, we can be
in the same place for four or five hours and say no

more than three words to each other, which is just the way we like it.

We've done a lot together, but some of my favourite memories come from our trip down Route 66 a few years ago, which I wrote about in *A Gentleman Abroad*. It's truly one of the great journeys, because it takes in so much of the States, from Chicago all the way to Santa Monica in California. Built in 1926, this road became known as the Main Street of America and is 3,940 kilometres in length, running through the states of Illinois, Missouri, Kansas, Oklahoma, Texas, New Mexico, Arizona and finally into California, where the route ends on Santa Monica Pier on the shores of the Pacific. You really get to see classic America, and in spite of all my visits to that country over the years, I'd never actually driven it.

My nieces and nephews had clubbed together to buy me the holiday for a significant birthday, and I knew that only Frank and I would be able to put up with each other in the RV, or campervan, for the 31-day journey. We had a fantastic time, and highlights of our trip included a visit to Andy Williams's theatre in Branson, Missouri. If you remember, Andy Williams sang 'Moon River' and a whole host of other classics in the 1970s and had a voice like syrup! Apparently, he got fed up touring and decided to build his very own theatre in the Ozarks, a picturesque area of forest and lakes that stretches across

Missouri, Oklahoma and Arkansas. It's since become famous because of the TV show *Ozark*, where an accountant and his wife relocate there and become major criminals.

Frank declared Branson to be 'like Bray on steroids'! Actually, Bray is a great deal more genteel. Branson is more like a sedate Las Vegas. Apart from Williams's Moon River Theatre, there are now over 50 other theatres with the likes of the Osmonds, Dionne Warwick and other classic singers performing regularly. We even saw billboards advertising Nathan Carter and Daniel O'Donnell! They come for a month each and fill a theatre of 600 seats twice or three times a day – I was told that they are very popular because of their clean-cut image. There are no punk rockers in Branson! Interestingly, the huge crowds that throng this surreal place are drawn from homes for the elderly and clubs all over the States – so that could be you, if you lived there! It really has to be seen to be believed. Mind you, there's strictly no drinking, because it's a very conservative place. Frank and I had a blast, even though it sometimes felt like a giant school concert!

Another highlight of our trip was in Amarillo, Texas, home to the Big Texan Steak Ranch. Built on Route 66 by a man called Bob Lee in the 1960s, it soon became an iconic stopping-off point for travellers, and the sign, held by a giant cowboy, became famous. Bob Lee was clearly a canny man, because when Route 66 was replaced by the new interstate in the 1970s, he had a bigger ranch restaurant built beside the motorway and moved the cowboy up there for good measure. He was obviously a born entrepreneur! Our RV stop was a short drive from the ranch, and they sent a huge limo bedecked in steer horns to bring us there! The driver told me that they take up to 600 people a day to the restaurant. We found it hard to believe, until we pulled up and discovered that the car park was full to bursting. There must have been at least 600 cars there. And, of course, the restaurant was huge – catering on an industrial scale!

We were ushered to our table in the gallery upstairs. It was covered in cowhide, and I couldn't help thinking that if you wanted to torture a vegetarian, you could bring them here! From this vantage point, we could look down on the main event: the 72-ounce-steak-eating contest. Three contestants sit up on a raised platform underneath three timers, and they have 60 minutes to eat a 72-ounce steak, with the winner getting their steak for free. That's four-and-a-half pounds or two kilos in new money. Can you imagine? The all-time champion of the event is a 120-pound woman who ate hers in 4 minutes and downed another one in 5. She must have a cast-iron constitution. My favourite bit of the evening, however, was being serenaded by two ancient cowboys. They informed us that they had once been a trio, but one of them had passed on. The older of the two had a giant double bass, bigger than himself, and they gamely belted out a country-and-western standard. It was really quite touching that these two elderly gentlemen were still giving it socks. There's no one else I'd rather have done the journey with than Frank. We've known each other for so long that we don't fuss about anything, nor do we mind each other's habits. We shared the driving and loved every moment of this classic journey. I thank God every day that our friendship has lasted so long.

Having said all of the above, I can sometimes feel lonely – everyone can. It might seem strange, but because I travel such a lot for work, I'm often on my own. Most of the time, I'm perfectly happy, but sometimes I long for a bit of company. All that travelling, setting up in a new city every couple of days, nights in different hotel rooms ... Even though I spend my days talking to people about Ireland, it's not the same as a chat with a friend. I'm always glad to get home to Kerry and reconnect with all the things I love. I've moved house recently, which I was dreading, so I'm actually in Kenmare now, in the middle of all the action, and that's made a huge difference to my life. I bump into people on the street all the time and stop for a chat, and the hotel is only around the corner. I'm sorry I didn't do it sooner.

– Life Happens –

A lot of people have talked to me about friendships and other relationships changing as they grow older. As we go through life, our status can change from married to widowed, or separated, or divorced, and we no longer fit into the comfortable couple world that we once did. Or we can find ourselves caring for an elderly relative, which means that we're unable to get out to socialise. Or, if we've been ill and at home for a while, it can be difficult to get out and about again. It might seem strange, when there are so many ways of keeping in touch nowadays, but perhaps WhatsApp and Facebook give us the impression that we're staying in touch, but what we're missing is real-life connection. Many of us learned this during the pandemic. I know that I did – Zoom is no replacement for an in-person chat!

We often hear that it's harder to maintain friendships or to make new ones when we get older, and the science actually backs this up. Apparently, we need 'continuous unplanned interaction and shared vulnerability' to make friendships, according to psychologist Marisa Franco. It's easy to see how this is possible at school and college or in a large office, where we're continually meeting new people, but when we're older and busier, this happens less. According to the same article in *Inc.* magazine, we need 200 hours to forge a friendship, and they can be hard to find. However, the good news is that if we organise ourselves a little bit, we can still make friends. This is actually more important as we age, because research shows us that older people with friends suffer less from cognitive decline and can live longer, happier lives.

We all know that loneliness is one of the diseases of the twenty-first century. According to a piece I read in *The Guardian* by George Monbiot a few years ago, 'Social isolation is as potent a cause of early death as smoking 15 cigarettes a day.' That's food for thought. Monbiot based his essay on the findings of Dr Julianne Holt-Lunstadt of Brigham Young University, who conducted a study review in 2010 called 'Social Relationships and Mortality Risk'. In it she discovered that loneliness can contribute to as much as a 30 per cent increase in stroke or heart disease, but 'the presence of a supportive person – or even thinking about them – can reduce cardio-vascular and neuroendocrine responses to stress'. According to the Campaign to End Loneliness (campaigntoendloneliness.org), social isolation leads to a 26 per cent rise in mortality. I won't go on! The idea is to be positive here, not to frighten the life out of you!

I think that we give ourselves an awfully hard time if we're lonely: it must be our fault, or we don't know how to make friends. But, on the plus side, we are better judges of character than we were when we were younger, and we also know what we like and what we don't, so we are better at zoning in on friendships that will really make a difference.

To me, the first job is to take the bull by the horns and be honest with ourselves if we're lonely. There's nothing to be ashamed of. Think about it and write it down if you need to. Are there particular situations in which you feel lonely? Is there a particular day of the week when the loneliness gets in on you? A lot of people tell me that the weekends can be difficult without the distraction of a busy office or family commitments. Other people tell me that their children leaving home can be a lonely time; others find the early days of retirement lonely, before they find new ways of making friends and enjoying their free time.

Once we've identified the problem, what can we do to make things better? Firstly, we need to go about things in a different way to when we were younger. We're less likely to meet people casually, so we might need to make it happen in a more organised way. And, while some of us are very good at small talk and enjoy it, perhaps you lack the confidence to get into conversation at the supermarket or bookshop. If that's the case, why not join a group in which you can share an interest? If you're into walking, join a walking group; if you're into classical music, become a friend of the National Concert Hall; if you like wine, find a local wine-tasting evening. If gardening is your thing, many counties have horticultural societies which you can join to share your passion for flowers or veg. This might seem obvious, but it works. Having a shared interest is an automatic ice breaker. For example, a friend of mine enjoyed sea swimming, but was a bit fed up going by herself. So she did some open-water swimming lessons last year and met a group of like-minded people with whom she now trains regularly. It's taking that initial step that can frighten some people – opening the door to a meeting place and seeing a group of strangers looking back at us! Again, there's nothing unusual about this – the chances are, other people are feeling the same way.

Have you heard the expression 'fake it until you make it'? That goes for making new friends. Stand up straight – as straight as you can at our age, anyway! – and smile. A smile goes a long way to making a connection. And don't be afraid to smile at your neighbours and say hello. They might be surprised and say hello back! And if they aren't friendly, don't feel too down about it. It's not you – they might have something else on their minds. Try again with another neighbour. They don't have to become your very best friend either: there's nothing more cheering than a friendly chat on the street. A friend of mine lived in London for a long time and led a busy life, so her neighbourhood was simply a place she returned to at night. However, when she was on maternity leave, she began to chat to local shopkeepers and people in the bank and post office – and they chatted back, to her surprise. She'd always thought that Londoners were reserved, but it turned out that all they needed was a little encouragement. So, go on, what's the worst that can happen?

The organisation Independent Age – www.independentage.org – has an excellent free guide on how to beat loneliness, with great practical advice, such as making sure to 'fill your diary' every week with events, no matter how small – a walk by the river, a trip to the shops. I know it might sound trivial, but it'll boost your confidence to see that you're getting out and about, in spite of what you might think. Another suggestion in this brilliant guide is to think positively and to write down things that you have done and that you're good at, to remind yourself that you have a lot going for you. If you're a card sharp or a cinephile, write it down. Sometimes, in the rush of life, we can forget what we really enjoy.

Looking after yourself is also important. If you're lonely, you can overeat, or fail to eat regular, nourishing meals. But you deserve it, and you'll feel much better about yourself if you take care of yourself. This reminds me of a cousin of mine who promised herself that she'd schedule a weekly wash and blow-dry at the hair salon when her kids left home and she had a little bit more money. It doesn't cost the earth, and every Friday she leaves the salon feeling at her very best. Looking after yourself doesn't have to mean buying a fur coat or shopping expensively. It can simply mean dressing properly, even if you're not going out, or scheduling an inexpensive treat like a cinema outing or even a trip to the library. Many community centres show films for older people, so you can rewatch *Casablanca* and cry!

Volunteering can be a great way of beating loneliness. Volunteer Ireland – www.volunteer.ie – has a list of volunteering opportunities in your area, everything from teaching to stewarding events to manning helplines and so on. And they really do need volunteers. The great thing is they are keen to nurture older volunteers, because they value their skills and experience.

I have mentioned getting a canine companion before, but you don't have to go the whole hog if it doesn't suit your lifestyle. Perhaps you'd consider fostering – taking in dogs or cats in need of TLC for a short while before they are adopted. You might volunteer at your local animal shelter, where you'll meet lots of like-minded individuals. But if you do want to get a pet, you'll quickly see the benefits. A pet will depend on you to look after it. For example, I met a man one day and we got chatting, then he revealed that he'd better hurry home because his pet parrot would give out to him if he was out for too long! There really is nothing better than the feeling that you are needed and wanted, is there? And the great thing about pets is you'll automatically make friends with other pet lovers – before you know it, a whole network will have opened up to you.

Dating for the Older Person

I write this with some trepidation, because I'm not an expert in the area by any means, but for those of us looking for a new relationship later in life, it can be a tricky subject. Thanks to my friends who have kindly shared their wisdom, I've learned a lot on the subject and hope that these few tips will be of help.

Dating in older life isn't straightforward, is it? We'll have been through a lot, probably, if we are widowed or divorced, and in all likelihood we won't have the confidence of youth. On the other hand, if we really are looking for Mr or Ms Right, we will persevere!

Of course, the landscape for dating has changed completely with the advent of online dating. For some of you, the prospect of creating a profile, putting a – realistic! – photo of yourself out there and generally tooting your own horn might feel awkward, particularly if the last time you'd put yourself out there was at the tennis-club hop! I'd suggest doing so with a friend, who knows what your best features are and will help you to draft a profile that reflects who you really are. If you're worried about online safety, pick a site that allows you to select your matches, don't share any details like your location or address and always meet somewhere busy and bustling.

On the plus side, if you aim at appropriate websites in terms of age and interests, you will automatically have narrowed the field. Ask any single friends which sites they use and do your own research. And be truthful about yourself. Don't say that you're a six-foot-five Adonis if you're a five-foot-four Michael from Tullamore. For a start, when you agree to meet, the truth will be clear, and, what's more, you might find that your date is more of a Michael-from-Tullamore fan! Instead, focus on what interests you. What's your favourite book? Are you a cat or a dog person? Are you a soccer or a GAA fan? What's your idea of a really nice day out, and so on? Being your real self will benefit you in the long run.

When it comes to dating online or IRL (in real life) after a long gap, your confidence may not be 100 per cent. Perhaps take up some confidence-boosting activities or interests, things that will make you feel at your best physically and mentally, and give yourself the time to recover before moving on with your life. You'll then be positive about this new direction and ready to take it on.

I was highly entertained to read a dating expert's advice to older people on Oprah's website. Her name was Bela Gandhi and she ran her own dating agency, so she should know, and apparently we older people are impatient! 'They want to check off a few boxes and have the perfect candidate arrive at their mailbox in 48 hours. It's important to be patient and to stay positive,' she says. 'Think of your frustration like a blizzard – it will do nothing but delay the delivery.' I love that!

In fact, remaining positive is the watchword here. You may find that you lose heart after being on a few dates, but if you look at them as opportunities to meet new people and learn new things, you can't go wrong. So what if you don't share someone's passion for geology or love of snail farming? There are plenty more out there who will share your interests. In fact, if dating online is too much for you, why not simply try going out with a friend to a buzzy restaurant or bar where, at the very least, you'll enjoy yourself?

The other key thing to remember is that, after a lifetime of experiences, you will know exactly who you are and what you want in life. But remember the blizzard above? Knowing who you are doesn't mean that you should pass right on after one date with someone promising. I've often heard it said, 'Oh, I didn't feel a spark.' After one date?! Could you be just a bit picky? Don't shoot the messenger, by the way: I'm just passing this on! Whatever approach you take, try to see it as fun and positive and that you are a person worthy of love and happiness. Everyone is. Good luck!

– Close Relationships –

As we grow older, our key relationships will change, there's no doubting this. It's part of life, really. We spend more time with partners due to retirement, and maybe we struggle to reconnect or our interests have diverged over the years. Perhaps we're letting children get on with the business of building their own lives and getting that empty-nest feeling; or we are at different stages in our lives than once-close friends. As with everything else, talking about it really helps.

As we grow older, we might think that we know our other half so well that we don't need to talk to them! But you might be surprised at what can emerge from a good chat – and a few plans to give your relationship a boost. For a start, how are you feeling in yourself? If you are feeling stale and a bit bored, you probably won't be filling your partner with excitement! What would you like to do to give your life some pep: take up a new hobby or learn a new skill? If you are bright and full of life, feeling fulfilled and engaged, your partner will see a new side to you and, hopefully, be intrigued. Change is really up to us, isn't it?

There's no doubting, however, that some other halves feel threatened by change. Sometimes, the status quo, no matter how unsatisfying, is more appealing than shaking things up. If that's the case, while you can't drag your partner along with you, you can talk about your need for change and excitement in your life. And you can take the first step, rather than expecting it automatically. When was the last time you bought your other half flowers? Probably when you were first dating! Or wrote them a letter – now, there's a challenge, when we can just text a heart emoji! It doesn't have to be something huge either, like the trip of a lifetime. A friend of mine stops off in her local bakery every now and then to buy her husband his favourite cake, for example, or she spots something she knows he'd like while she's out and about and puts it to one side. Little reminders of your love and devotion can make everyone feel happy. And remember, there are lots of different ways to show your affection and care. Many people prefer to do practical things for their loved ones, like putting up shelves or driving them to an appointment and waiting for them after. It's all about what works for you and yours.

And what about your hobbies? You might assume that your other half isn't interested in your flower-arranging club, for example, or your amateur dramatics production, but if you tell him or her about it, you might be surprised – they might well like to hear about something new and fresh. Or, even if they don't, you'll appreciate the effort they've made to look interested! Someone I've known for a long time is married to a man who loves hiking more than anything else in the world. It's his passion. Now, she's not into rambling herself, but she finds that if she listens and takes an interest, he appreciates the effort, even if he knows it's not her thing. And she gets to tell him all about her bridge playing in return ... I believe it's called quid pro quo!

A lot of things happen to us as we get older that can change our relationships. Ill health might lead us to re-evaluate our priorities and might leave those close to us feeling left out. Talk to your other half, and not just about household chores. Ask them honestly how they feel about the illness, what you can both do to adapt to your changing lives and how you can move forward together. Perhaps an illness wasn't something you'd planned for, but acceptance will go a long way to helping you both to forge a new path.

I'm well aware that caring for a loved one can change a dynamic, and for carers particularly self-care is important. I know, easier said than done, but it's difficult to care for someone else if you're not caring for yourself. Organisations like Family Carers

Ireland (www.familycarers.ie) can be of help, organising coffee mornings and giving advice on financial and social supports, and they also have a helpline: 1800 240 724. Also, organisations like the Alzheimer Society of Ireland have helplines for carers, as well as information and support – 1800 341 341.

If you're finding it hard to communicate with your beloved, don't assume that it's impossible. You might be a bit rusty, but you can still sit down together, for example, to watch a TV programme that you both enjoy – my friend's mother and her husband sit down every evening at 5.30 to watch *Pointless*. It can be a stress-free way of spending time together. Remember, you don't have to make a big deal about it – you can have a chat in the car, where people don't feel as pressured, or while out for a walk. Use 'I' words if you can, rather than 'you'. For example, 'I find our rows about what to watch on the TV frustrating', rather than 'You really annoy me hogging the remote control to watch football'. Avoid blaming the other person, even if you feel annoyed with them, because they'll immediately get defensive. And if you are tackling a tricky subject, acknowledge that – we don't all have the same views, thankfully, or else the world would be a very boring place.

– Boomeranging –

Many people have spoken to me about the issues that come with having adult children still living at home – something many of us face nowadays with the housing crisis and young people studying for extra qualifications. It's a new dilemma for many: when I was 18, I left home, never to return, as did most of my brothers and sisters, leaving only John at home with Mum. Now, we talk about the 'boomerang' generation, where children leave for a couple of years to travel or study then bounce back to us! What's more, many adult children return home, often with babies in tow, to save for a deposit on a home. All of this can put pressure on older people as retirement plans are shelved and finances are stretched, not to mention issues around personal space and privacy.

So, how can we tackle this subject while assuring our children that we still love them? Based on my conversations with friends who are parents, I have a few tips:

- Before they move back in, have a chat with them about how long they expect to be staying, whether or not you will be looking for a contribution to bills and what chores you might reasonably expect them to do. They aren't children any more!
- If you're no longer a 'parent' with a capital 'P', how would you like the house to run? Most of

us wouldn't want to find ourselves making big dinners like we did when they were small, so how about a rota? A friend of mine has one – everyone cooks one night a week and it's brilliant. They eat all kinds of interesting things (some more successful than others!) and the burden is lifted from Mum and Dad. The same applies to chores: get everyone to do one particular chore and stick to it.

- Don't do things for your adult children that they can do themselves. You might have washed their clothes when they were six, but they can do it now. The same goes for emptying their bins or cleaning up after a party.

- Respect their privacy. You don't need to know what's happening in their lives in every detail – and some things you might not want to know – so no wandering into their bedrooms and no snooping.

- Make sure that you have your own space. If you can't get any peace and quiet at home, head out for a walk or a coffee so that you can have a chat.

Books about Friendship and Relationships

Sometimes, reading can reveal surprising things to us, entertain and provoke us, or make us laugh or dream. Here's a selection of my favourites on the subject of friendship and love.

A Man Called Ove – Fredrik Backman. This made me laugh out loud, and at the same time it's really heartwarming, as grumpy Ove comes to love his neighbours and get over the death of his wife. Friendship can get you through anything is its central message.

Eleanor Oliphant Is Completely Fine – Gail Honeyman. I read this during lockdown and it really gave me hope and joy, as well as being a quirky read. Eleanor is shy and socially awkward, but thanks to the friendship of colleague Raymond, she learns to live a little and to deal with her past.

Emma – Jane Austen. I love this book about meddling but well-meaning friends! Emma is only dying to set her best friend up with a suitor, and in the process makes a hash of it all and learns a valuable lesson about the power of good intentions. I also enjoyed the movie, starring a young Gwyneth Paltrow with a very convincing English accent.

The Kite Runner – Khaled Hosseini. One of those absolute heartbreakers, about a childhood friendship between Amir and Hassan that is broken by war, and Amir's attempt to fix it. Apparently, Hosseini got the idea for the novel from a story he read about the banning of kite-flying in Afghanistan, which is a very popular hobby there.

The Gathering – Anne Enright. This might seem a more 'traditional' novel about family, but it's anything but, as a dysfunctional family gathers to remember the life of a son and brother, and a sister guards a dark family secret. I think Enright is one of the best writers about family.

Midwinter Break – Bernard McLaverty. I loved this story about a long-married elderly couple on a winter holiday. I particularly enjoyed the couple's 'ailment hour', in which they gave themselves one hour only per day to discuss their ailments! Sound familiar?

Silver Wedding – Maeve Binchy. An oldie but most definitely a goodie. I loved these interlinking stories about a couple and their guests getting ready for their 25th wedding anniversary celebration. Binchy was such a brilliant observer of human beings.

Fleishmann Is in Trouble – Taffy Brodesser-Akner. I thoroughly enjoyed this novel about a man reeling from the breakdown of his marriage. It's very New York, but very funny too.

5.
Family with a Capital 'F'

'Families is where our nation finds hope.
Where wings take dream [sic].'

George W. Bush

As I write this chapter, it's almost Christmas and I'm buying presents for my nieces and nephews and looking forward to a busy time at the hotel. I'm wondering which house I'll go to for Christmas dinner or whether I'll host it myself to christen my new home: a good dilemma, because this can be a lonely time of year for so many of us. I feel that I'm very lucky. It seems like just the right time to write about family, though, because we consider the season to be a family one.

Forgive me if I'm repeating myself, but it's true that, like so many things, our relationships with our families can change as we grow older. This isn't necessarily a bad thing: it's just part of life. We might find our children suddenly parenting us, for example! We might lose a sibling and find ourselves growing close to their children, feeling parental responsibility for them. We might be close to a brother or sister when younger but grow apart from them as we go through different life stages. Also, those of us who are single feel differently about family occasions. We do want to be part of them, of course, but we don't want people to feel that they have to invite us! At this stage in life, everyone has settled into their roles, so it can be difficult sometimes to work out what our role is. But with some thought and understanding, we can all navigate tricky times as a family and, most importantly, enjoy the relationships we have with our nearest and dearest.

The word 'family' can mean different things to different people. Interestingly, many dictionaries define it in the traditional sense. The *Cambridge Dictionary* describes family as 'a group of people who are related to each other, such as a mother, a father, and their children'. For the *Oxford Learner's Dictionary*, a family is 'a group consisting of one or two parents and their children'. That's quite a narrow definition these days. Interestingly, the Central Statistics Office in Ireland says that 'For census purposes, a family is defined as a couple with or without children, or a one-parent family with one or more children'. That's quite a broad definition and demonstrates that 'family' can come in many shapes and sizes. For some, it means one parent and child; for others, it means an extended family of all generations and all relationships, from grandparents to cousins to siblings. In fact, until the arrival of the 'nuclear' family after World War II, most people lived in extended families, with grandparents or an aunt or uncle living with a couple and their children. Newlyweds often moved in with the in-laws while they were saving for a home, and Granny or Grandad often came to live with a family when he or she got older.

The nuclear family is a relatively recent invention, but even that is changing now. For many of us, 'family' can mean two people who are married or in a committed relationship, but who may not have children. Or a group of people that you know very well but who aren't blood relations. Perhaps you got to know them when you first moved out of home or in your first job; if you've been working in a place for a long time, as I have, your colleagues can be like family. Fundamentally, 'family' is whatever you define it to be.

Having said that, whatever shape your family takes, it probably has its ups and downs, and old age can really change family relationships. If you're a son or daughter, your parents, who seemed almost super-human when you were a small child, are now old and may be fragile mentally or physically. That can come as a shock to some of us. If we're not careful, we can begin to find ourselves bossing them about and telling them what's good for them! It's important to remember that our parents are still grown-ups, even though they might be frail. I met a friend for coffee recently, and she was telling me about her parents, who were just about managing at home, as they were both in their late 80s. She had that conversation in her head about them possibly needing to go into a home and discussed it with her siblings, but when she broached the subject with her mother, her mother said, 'Well, I know I might eventually need to go in to a home, but I don't want it to be the end of the road.' My friend immediately understood her mother's point of view and was glad that she'd asked.

Unsurprisingly, most people in Ireland would like to remain in their own homes when they're old. Indeed, when I read an article by Arthur Beesley in the *Irish Times* last year on the subject, it was clear that the government hopes that this will be the pre-ferred model in the future. I suppose it makes sense when you have an ageing population. Remember the statistics from Chapter 2? By 2050, according to Beesley's article, 27 per cent of us will be over 65, so it will be quite a lot cheaper for us to remain at home with the right supports.

Thankfully, day centres, which provide such valuable support to older people living at home, have now reopened after Covid. In fact, I bumped into an elderly neighbour recently on her way to the day centre. 'Oh, that's nice,' I said, when she told me where she was going. 'You must enjoy being looked after for the day.' She was most offended. 'I help out at the day centre!' she said indignantly. 'I serve the teas and coffees to the old dears.' You're only as old as you feel!

You'll be glad to know that the government has pledged extra money and legislation to make home care the priority, but there will still be a need for residential care for those of us who have illnesses such as dementia. Making that decision is never easy, and it can often result in family conflict. One daughter or son will feel that Mum or Dad needs support before their illness progresses too far, but the other won't agree and so on. Naturally, the decision comes with a lot of guilt – it's perfectly normal. You want to do your very best for your mum or dad. And if you are Mum or Dad, you will of course have mixed feelings about this next stage, rather like my friend's mother, above.

How will you know when the time is right, however? It really will depend. It might be never, and your parent will be hale and hearty, like my mother. Or you might find yourself dealing with such physical or cognitive decline that it's obvious your parent needs extra support. Maybe they will have had a fall or two and be unable to recover. Maybe they will show signs that they have memory issues, such as leaving the stove on or the front door open. There might be problems getting dressed or showered or remembering to pay bills.

What my friend learned was the importance of discussing next steps while her parents were feeling relatively well. That way, everyone can look at the available options and decide what might be best when it's needed. You don't want to be scrambling for a place when your parent is in urgent need of one. In the meantime, you might find that your parents can manage at home for a little bit longer with the right supports. If that is the case, your public health nurse or hospital social worker is the next port of call.

If you're an elderly person, thinking about residential care will probably give you the shivers, but it need not if you are part of the decision-making process and have already discussed it with loved ones. Have a good look at the facilities and what each offers and try not to assume that they'll be awful. No, they won't be home, but perhaps they will offer you something else? The Health Information and Quality Authority – www.hiqa.ie – carries out inspections and reports on residential homes, so you can check them.

Some of us might even welcome the sociability of a group setting. I found this a surprising thought until a cousin of mine told me about her mother, who had been widowed at the age of 75 and still lived alone on the family farm. When she got to 80, she checked herself into the local home for the elderly and said, 'It was the best decision I ever made.' Many of her neighbours and friends were already there, so she had a ready-made social circle and thoroughly enjoyed all of the group activities and the security that came with having someone on-site in case of emergencies.

The reality is, no matter what we do or decide, relationships at this stage can really benefit from thought and conversation and an understanding that, while us older folk might be, well, older, we still want to be in charge of our lives as much as possible.

Jokes about Families

Families aren't all doom and gloom, in spite of what Tolstoy said in *Anna Karenina*: 'Happy families are all alike; every unhappy family is unhappy in its own way.' Here are a few jokes about this institution that will hopefully make you laugh.

A man and his wife were sitting in the living room discussing a living will. 'Just so you know, I never want to live in a vegetative state, dependent on some machine and fluids from a bottle. If that ever happens, just pull the plug,' the man says. His wife got up, unplugged the TV and threw out all the beer.

My dad died because we couldn't remember his blood type. As he died, he kept insisting for us to 'be positive', but it's hard without him.

What did Darwin's son tell his siblings?
You're adapted!

Good moms let you lick the beaters.
Great moms turn them off first.

My kids have been throwing Scrabble tiles at each other again. It's all fun and games until someone loses an i.

First woman: 'My son came to visit for summer vacation.'
Second woman: 'How nice! Did you meet him at the airport?'
First woman: 'Oh, no. I've known him for years!'

My family has a tradition of placing bets on how high they can hoist my mother's sister each Christmas at the family get-together. I keep telling them to stop, as it will end in disaster, but they just keep upping the ante each year.

− Family Conflicts −

'The strength of a family,
like the strength of an army,
is in its loyalty to each other.'

Mario Puzo

For those of you who might not be familiar with the name, Mario Puzo was the author of *The Godfather*. Thankfully, most families aren't killing each other all the time like the Corleones − at least, not literally − but I think he's right. Sticking together makes family work. If we fall out with each other, we're not half as strong on our own. Still, coming together as a family is often not straightforward. We have an awful habit of remembering things that our siblings did to us when we were six years of age and bringing it up when we're sixty! We can also harbour resentments about parents treating us unequally or one of us having more responsibility than others. The pitfalls are seemingly endless!

So, how do we stick together as a family when we are older or when we have older relatives to look after?

It's easy for me to talk about sharing the responsibility for your parents' care when they need it, but I know that Susan and Kate, my two sisters, did so much for Mum. She'd spend Christmas at the Park Hotel, Kenmare, and we always tried to divide our time with her equally, but sometimes life and work got in the way. And, to be honest, many women take on the lion's share of caring for elderly relatives. In case you doubt me, I've studied the statistics! It probably used to be the case that women worked less outside the home, but that's no longer true, so, gents, it's time to do your bit. Try to divide up the tasks as evenly as possible and according to people's skills. Perhaps one of you is a brilliant organiser and another might be great at getting parents out and about. The important thing is to share the responsibility as equally as you can to avoid resentment. No matter what's happening or how stressful it all is, try to keep the lines of communication open.

And when you're the oldie in question? I have learned that there are as many different types of relationships as there are families out there! I work with one of my brothers, so we couldn't be closer, and I'm frequently in Sligo visiting my other brother and sister, but I am aware that siblings aren't always close. Things like unspoken resentment, a sense of unfairness or a simple misunderstanding can push them apart. Even so, your siblings can be a source of support when your parents have gone, and of shared memories. Someone once said to me that he knew who he was because of his siblings, and I see what he meant. Maybe you fought like cats and dogs when you were younger, but hopefully you'll have ironed that out by the time you reach 70! It takes work, though ...

One excellent tip to building sibling trust and empathy is to make time for each other separate from your parents. This is because the minute we gather around the kitchen table we have a habit of regressing to our childhood selves! If we meet our siblings for a coffee or a trip to the movies, we can be our grown-up selves and enjoy the experience. I have a friend who takes a holiday with her sister every year. They're very different, but on holiday they can just be silly and have fun together, and it has really strengthened their bond.

One thing she suggested to me was not to hang onto old stuff with your siblings. 'I remember the time you pulled my hair when we were five.' You're not five any more – at least, not physically, so perhaps you can gently let go of that. However, depending on the age gap, your sibling will have different memories of growing up to the ones you have and different experiences. Have a chat about them, without beating each other up about it, so you can gain a better understanding of your sibling's point of view. That's key to having a healthy relationship – being able to understand how a sibling feels, even if it seems unreasonable or puzzling to us.

I came across a website in the UK for a charity called Stand Alone, which supports people who are estranged from their families. They run support groups for those estranged and conduct research on the issue. This really brought it home to me just how much of a problem it can be. No matter what, try not to fall out with a sibling. We all know from a certain royal memoir what the cost can be, and it's heartbreaking. Even if you have had a row, try not to close the door on your relationship with them permanently. Keep the lines of communication open, even if it's just a quick text or phone call, or a postcard from a holiday destination. You never know when you might need each other. And for those older folk with children, please God make a will and make it fair! What might seem obvious to you as a parent – say, giving a single child your home because your married child has one already – might seem like unfairness to your children, as if you're favouring one over the other. Try to divide your estate equally – your children will see it as dividing your love for them equally. Even better, write your will and share it with them while you're alive, so that everyone knows where they stand.

Communication is essential in families, but how this works is really down to each family. It's important to respect your family's style when communicating. For example, wading into a situation and insisting on a family meeting when you've never had one in your lives isn't the best idea. Nor might gathering everyone in the same room for a chat, as some people might feel they are being put on the spot. If you have something to discuss, try to keep things as relaxed as you can and focus on the now – not on what happened 40 years ago.

My new favourite word is 'boundaries'. It might sound very American, but setting boundaries with loved ones is perfectly acceptable – I'd argue that it's essential. If Mum keeps ringing you during your Monday board meeting, explain to her that you can't talk at that time, but that you'd be very happy to chat later. Give her a time when you'll call and stick to it. Also, respect your adult children's boundaries if you are older. Try to understand that bathtime and bedtime will be very busy for them if they have children, so don't pick that moment to call! If in doubt, just ask, 'What's the best time for me to call?' And don't turn up on their doorstep, all set to sit down on the sofa and have a nice cup of tea – not unless you plan to make them dinner or put their children to bed for them anyway. People are busy nowadays, so arrange things in advance. And talk about things. Ask your daughter if she's okay with a call on a Friday evening or if she'd prefer a Tuesday; if she'd like to hear from you more often than once a week – or less! Nobody is a mind-reader, so if in doubt, just ask.

– Granny and Grandad –

I still remember my summers with Granny and Grandad on their farm in County Sligo. They were wonderful days, feeding the hens and bringing bottles of tea and fruitcake up to the fields when the hay was being brought in. I used to love to watch my grandfather shaving himself in the yard outside – there was no indoor bathroom! – and helping Granny with the chores. It was such a simple, relaxed way of life, and I treasure the memories. It's easy to see why grandparents are so important to children – and children to grandparents.

Many of my friends have told me that the arrival of grandchildren has been one of the greatest pleasures of their lives. They can enjoy the wonder of watching a child grow up, and they often have more time to spend with their grandchildren than they did when their own children were young. What's more, they can do all of the things they loved doing with their own children, like reading a bedtime story, having a painting party, baking and so on. And, as the saying goes, you can give them back at the end of the day! You can share all kinds of different experiences with your grandchild, and even learn a thing or two. However, becoming Granny or Grandad is a big life change and, like any, needs a bit of thought. Even if you think you know it all already!

I've tried to be part of my nieces' and nephews' lives since they were born. Watching them grow up and seeing them become the fine adults they are has been wonderful. Many of my suggestions below are based on my own experience, but I've also asked friends who are grandparents for their advice.

One of the first suggestions was to have a good, long think about what kind of a grandparent you want to be. Be honest with yourself: will you want to see your grandchildren every day of the week? Would you like to have them for the summer holidays or do you have other plans? Do you plan to offer babysitting services on a regular basis, or do you feel that your work is done, having raised your own family? Don't offer to babysit one or two days a week or to drop them to creche and then back out of it – best to have thought it through first and offer what you know you will be happy with.

If you're tempted to get involved as a new grandparent, great, but respect the boundaries. Don't offer unsolicited advice. In fact, only give advice if you're specifically asked for it. And try not to say things like 'in my day ...'. A friend of mine always laughed when her mother told her that babies should be left outdoors in their prams under a tree, just as she had been at the same age. Modern parents are a bit more involved and that's just fine.

Parenting styles vary hugely from generation to generation, so be prepared for your son or daughter to have different ideas about bringing up baby. In our day, children were seen and not heard, and that's not the case today, where children are freer to enjoy and express themselves. We may not approve, but it's no longer our business. The same applies to weaning, sleeping practices, eating habits and so on. And as for names, if your new grandchild is called after someone in *Game of Thrones*, you'll just have to suck it up! Your role is to support the new parents, not to undermine them.

It's tempting to buy all around you when there's a grandchild on the way, but before you splash the cash, ask the parents-to-be what they'd like. Maybe they'd love you to buy a pram or a changing table, but they might not need a sterilising set or plush toys. And even if you've kept your son's childhood cot, don't be offended if he doesn't want it for his own child. It might not be up to modern-day safety specifications, for example.

Think about how you can help the parents of a newborn – say that you'd like to pop by with a bag of ready meals to put in the freezer, for example. And don't be afraid to ask, 'What can I do?' A friend of mine said her mother came over and emptied the laundry basket, putting on washes and drying everything, which was a godsend. Another was thrilled when Granny came over to take the baby for a walk while she napped. As the support act, make yourself useful without being obtrusive.

Respect your children's rules for their offspring: if they say 'no sugar', don't fill the children with jelly babies or other sugary treats. If they are vegan, so what? Thankfully, there are lots of options in the supermarket. On the other hand, children love visits to Granny and Grandad precisely because there will be treats! Check with Mum or Dad if it's okay to give them a little something after dinner or if they're well behaved.

Avoiding Family Conflict over Wills

I listened to a heartrending piece by Ryan Tubridy on his show last year, discussing the pain and conflict that can be caused over inheritance of the family farm. It was clear that the children of farmers who hadn't benefitted from the will felt left out and ignored and resented the way in which they had to carve out their lives, while the sibling who inherited had a life handed to him or her – but the person who inherited also inherited the weight of the parents' expectations. All the views made so much sense, and I wondered at the time if there was any way to avoid conflict over inheritance. Here are a few things to consider:

- Did you know that only three in ten Irish people have made a will? That's an awful lot of family squabbles waiting to happen. So, start with that.
- Discuss your plans with your family in advance. Don't leave them to fight over things when you're gone. Tell them why you've done what you've done so that there will be no guesswork later. You might not enjoy the fallout, but it's so much healthier to have it all out in the open when you're alive.
- Appoint your executor with care. You might decide that you'd like to share the job equally between your children, but if you have six of them, that's six voices to listen to. Appoint someone you know will be calm and fair and able to make objective decisions.
- Try to understand that, while you might not see your bequests as personal slights, your children/ relatives might well see it as such.
- Don't make promises you don't intend to keep. No telling cousin Joan that the Ming vase on the mantelpiece is hers unless you plan to say so in your will. Some people do use wills emotionally, promising cash or assets that don't end up being left to the person to whom they were promised, and that's to be avoided.
- Keep your will up to date. You never know when circumstances might change. Say your spouse dies and you remarry and have more children

but fail to update your will – your younger children might be left out. Citizens Information – www.citizensinformation.ie – has a full section on deaths and wills.

– Family Occasions –

'Before I got married,
I had six theories about bringing up children.
Now, I have six children and no theories.'

John Wilmot

Some families like nothing better than a good old family get-together. For others, they're a nightmare! In fact, when I was researching this section, I kept coming across advice on 'surviving' family gatherings, which tells me that lots of people find them tricky. If your family is in the first category – that is, get-together fans – be sure to schedule a couple of gatherings every year, like a summer barbecue, an Easter picnic or a casual lunch at someone's house, with everyone taking a turn. Talk about get-togethers on your family WhatsApp, such as Uncle Joe's birthday or a christening, to make sure that you can all make it – and divide up the tasks. Make sure that you see each other regularly and enjoy the time you spend together.

Often, siblings are held together by their parents as they get older, but what happens if they pass away? Then it'll fall to you all to make the effort to stay in touch. Try your very best to do so. Don't assume that others will do it, now that Mum or Dad has gone. Put yourself in charge of the family WhatsApp group and suggest a get-together every now and then. It can be difficult nowadays, with people living all over the world, but why not schedule a FaceTime or Zoom call every now and then to keep the connection going? I know Covid has probably put us off them, but I think they were brilliant at keeping us all in touch when we couldn't see each other.

Some people like to organise their get-togethers for maximum fun, particularly if all the generations will be there. It's certainly a good idea to have something to amuse the children while you get a bit of peace and quiet. A treasure hunt can be fun or an Easter-egg hunt – anything involving chocolate is a winner. A badminton net, paddling pool or games set-up will be handy if you're outside, as will a couple of footballs or a sandpit. However, do check that your garden is child friendly before you invite the grandchildren over. Ponds or water features are a magnet for little ones, so be sure to either block access to them or install a pond cover while they're visiting. In fact, if water is involved, *ensure that an adult is always present to supervise*. Keep things like bird feeders out of reach (you'd be surprised what children will eat!) and put your garden tools away in the shed. If you'll be indoors, check for things that will be in reach of little fingers, and if you don't want them broken, put them away. If your dog or cat isn't a small-child lover, ask the neighbours if they'd be able to mind them for the afternoon. (The pet, that is, not the child!) If you'd prefer to head out for the day, pick a venue that will work for everyone: a picnic in the woods or a day at the beach, rather than a visit to a stately home.

If your fun will be indoors, games are always good to get everyone together. Simple card games, like 21 or snap or gin rummy, can be fun, as can classic games like Twister or Monopoly (you can adjust it for the patience of those involved!). Pictionary is always good, as is Who Am I? where you have to guess the name written on the Post-it stuck to your forehead. Joke telling is also fun – when the jokes are age-appropriate, of course – and time-sensitive games like 30 Seconds will always guarantee just the right level of hysteria!

If you're in the latter category, and family get-togethers are a minefield, remember, they aren't obligatory. You don't have to entertain relatives if you don't get on – there's no law that insists you do so. However, many of us want to at least keep on good terms with our families, even if we find the occasions difficult, so we will extend an invitation to a get-to-gether – through gritted teeth!

Some of us older folk find multi-generational gatherings a bit exhausting. Perhaps it's because we feel that we're expected to behave in a certain way? But there's no need to throw the doors open every Sunday for a roast dinner and be disappointed when the grandchildren get restless or their parents have to keep getting up from the table to attend to them. Set the bar a great deal lower and invite them over for tea and cake, or a cup of coffee in the afternoon, or a teatime picnic in the garden – anything that's relaxed and unfussy and doesn't demand too much of anyone.

If Aunty Joan is a nightmare, but you still have to invite her over, keep the visit short. Lunch, not dinner; afternoon tea, not a four-course tasting menu! And have an exit strategy – a meeting or an outing to go to. No, this isn't rude – you're simply protecting yourself from unnecessary stress, and you need to do that.

Some people find that inviting an unpleasant relative is easier in a crowd – a drinks party or a barbecue where they'll be drowned out by the noise! Others find that a neutral space, such as a hotel or pub, is a great place to meet badly behaved family members, because they will be on their best behaviour in a public place.

If your issue is with a close family member, this can be very painful and difficult. Can you think of anything that you like about them? Something that might redeem them just a bit and make the visit go more smoothly? Or can you find it in your heart to empathise with their situation? Perhaps Aunty Joan is a bit unpleasant because her husband died and she hates being alone, or perhaps your sister acts up because she feels insecure about her status? Empathising with them doesn't mean that you are condoning their behaviour, just trying to put it in context. For example, a good friend of mine knows that her sister says unpleasant things and tries to provoke rows when she is upset. Naturally, my friend doesn't like this behaviour, but she understands the reason for it – her sister's anxiety about something. Sometimes, she chooses to let the barbs go right over her head, but at others she says, 'I can sense you're upset. What's the problem?' And, lo and behold, her sister will tell her! Sometimes, people want to be understood, but they go the wrong way about it.

Communication When a Person Has Changed

Sometimes it can be difficult to talk to an elderly family member due to the sad fact that they have an illness such as dementia. It can be bewildering and disconcerting for those of us close to them, not to mention what it must be like for them. If you have seen the excellent film *The Father*, starring Anthony Hopkins, you will gain some understanding of how confusing the onset of dementia can be for those who experience it. It's well worth watching.

If you have dementia, or know someone who does, www.understandtogether.ie has some excellent resources to help you manage the condition. I found the section on living well with dementia very interesting because, quite honestly, I hadn't thought of it in such positive terms. According to them, there's a lot you can do to live with your condition as comfortably as possible. For a start, they suggest that having a manageable routine is important: they stress the importance of having reminders, to-do lists, wallcharts or whiteboards to write the reminders on and organisers for your medications; they also have great suggestions for communicating, including meeting people in familiar, comfortable environments and not being afraid to ask people to remind you of their names, if needed. Thankfully, according to this helpful information, 'A diagnosis of dementia doesn't mean giving up everything; in fact being physically and socially active is really good for you. Stay in touch with your friends, family and community. Keep up your hobbies – maybe even take up some new ones.' They also emphasise the importance of taking exercise; you don't have to climb Mont Blanc, though. A simple walk in nature every day will be brilliant. To find out more about this joint initiative of the HSE and the Alzheimer Society, check the website or phone: 1800 341 341.

There's no doubting that when it comes to caring for us older folk, many people in this country are our informal carers and supports. According to Family Carers, that could be as many as half a million people. Their head of communications and policy, Catherine Cox, says, 'We now estimate that family carers save the State in excess of €20bn every year. They reduce the pressure on our hospital beds by keeping loved ones at home, where they wish to be, and keep them safe.' That's a wonderful thing, but it also highlights just how much family members and friends do.

If you are worried about a loved one living with dementia, there are a few helpful things that you can do.

- At an early stage, you can talk to them freely and help to prepare them for what may lie ahead, including the kind of care that they may need as their disease progresses. This is important, as is getting any paperwork in order while they are still well.
- Early on in the disease, they may still be able to live independently, with your help. Don't forget to contact your local public health nurse for advice and support. Ask them to arrange a home visit to assess needs. They will carry out a care needs

assessment to see what services might benefit your relative. Meanwhile, focus on simple things that might help them, such as writing reminders on Post-its to switch off appliances, and check that your loved one has remembered to eat. Sometimes they can forget. Discuss their condition with your GP along with them, if possible, so that they understand as much as they can about their disease and if medication can slow its progress.

- Explore support groups such as Dementia Ireland – www.dementiaireland.com – and the Alzheimer Society of Ireland – www.alzheimer.ie. Also, the Irish Dementia Working Group is made up of people experiencing dementia – who better to understand their condition?

- Be patient if you possibly can – it can be very difficult if you have to answer the same question repeatedly, but try to understand that this is the disease, not the person being difficult. If you need a moment, take it. I have a friend whose father suffers from memory problems, and he went into hospital recently for a procedure. After the procedure had been performed, he was adamant that nothing whatsoever had happened. This might seem amusing, but he had to be reminded any number of times what the procedure was and that he was, in fact, in recovery. My friend did laugh, though, that he was feeling so much better and had no recollection of his surgery ... silver linings!

- Don't be afraid to use visual cues to help your relative to remember pleasant occasions in their past. Many places use 'reminiscence therapy' to help people enjoy their memories through songs and images. A friend of mine used to go to a choir for people living with dementia and their carers with her mother, and it gave them both great pleasure.

- Keep things quiet and calm – no loud TV or radio or chatter to upset them – and if this means what you might feel are awkward silences, don't worry. The chances are that your loved one will be quite content, even if it's hard for you.

- Don't try to cope alone with this disease – it's not possible. Reach out to any support services or helpful relatives or community groups. Lean on them and don't be apologetic about it. You are dealing with something life-changing and you will need support and compassion.

Of course, your loved one might not have dementia but might be physically limited due to something like Parkinson's disease or simple old age. They may need help getting dressed, showering, getting into bed and taking medications. Your local health centre or public health nurse will advise you on getting a carer to help out with some of these tasks so that you have a little less on your plate.

Fun for All the Family

From the above, you might well think that old age is a cascade of disease and difficulty. Of course, for many people it has its challenges, but it's not a litany of doom and gloom. A lot depends on how well you are, of course, but even with illness you can still connect and have fun! It's useful to spend time with younger people and to be reminded that life can still be very happy. Why not gather on the sofa with a bowl of popcorn to watch one of these movies?

My Cousin Vinnie is a firm favourite in my family. It's a classic fish-out-of-water story in which Joe Pesci has to represent two clients on a murder charge, having only just passed his bar exam – on the fifth attempt!

Up – I love this animated movie about the touching relationship between an elderly man mourning the death of his wife and a funny little boy – the subject matter might be serious, but the laughs keep coming.

Home Alone – a friend tells me that her children watched this on a loop when they were small, but the idea of a child left behind by his family at Christmas captures the imagination and the slapstick is fantastic.

The Wizard of Oz – I'm putting this in for my friend Anne, who had to be removed from the school gym and taken home during a showing because she was so terrified of the Wicked Witch of the West!

Encanto is a lovely story about a Colombian family written by *Hamilton*'s Lin-Manuel Miranda – no one could fail to be enchanted by it.

The Princess Bride has romance, great jokes and fine battle scenes – something for everyone!

Elf – I still laugh out loud every time I watch this movie about a half-elf, half-human, played by Will Ferrell.

Cool Runnings – this film about Jamaica's bobsleigh team that took part in the Winter Olympics of 1988 is both funny and heartwarming.

I loved Steven Spielberg's *The Fablemans*, which I watched in New York earlier this year. It's a lovely family movie.

– Sandwiched –

When I left home at 18, the only person left at home in Sligo was John, who was still going to school at that stage. The rest of us were all out working or studying, including Mum, who had returned to the civil service following Dad's death. Nowadays, the picture looks very different, which is why some of you will have heard of the Sandwich Generation. This is the generation of middle-aged people with elderly parents and, at the same time, children or adults still living at home. If you're wondering about the relevance to you as an older person, it's good to know just how much your sons and daughters care – and for two different generations! And with people living for so much longer, some of you younger oldies might be sandwiched yourselves. Perhaps understanding more about this unique set of challenges will be helpful to you.

According to the Irish Longitudinal Study on Ageing, undertaken by TCD in 2013:

- 'Half of all sandwich generation women provide substantial time support to their parents, one-third provide support towards basic and personal care such as dressing, eating and bathing (activities of daily living) for an average of 21 hours per week and more than half give household help with chores, transportation and shopping (instrumental activities of daily living).'

- 'One-third of the sandwich generation women provide practical household help including shopping and household chores to their non-resident adult children for an average of 12 hours per month.'

- 'One-third of sandwich generation women look after their grandchildren for an average of 34 hours per month.'

That makes for eye-opening reading. And, just in case you think that this problem is unique to Ireland, in America, according to Pew Research, 'Nearly half

(47 per cent) of adults in their 40s and 50s have a parent age 65 or older and are either raising a young child or financially supporting a grown child (age 18 or older). And about one-in-seven middle-aged adults (15 per cent) is providing financial support to both an aging parent and a child.'

When you think about it, these statistics really do seem daunting – particularly for women, who provide the majority of care to relatives. It's a fact! According to the CSO, 60.9 per cent of carers were women in 2016, compared with 39.5 per cent men. But we can't change society, at least not overnight, so we have to work out how to live with this complex role as we age – or, indeed, if we're already living with it. Thankfully, there are some things we can do to make this tricky balancing act easier and keep our sanity in the process.

The word 'self-care' might make you groan if you're a carer. Maybe you're wondering where on earth you'd get the time for a manicure or a shopping expedition. But might you have time for a brisk walk around the block, or to wash and blow-dry your hair? Can you set aside just 20 minutes a day to do something you enjoy, even if it's just reading a magazine? Little and often seems to work for many of my friends who look after others to avoid burnout. Recently, I read an interview with the writer Kate Mosse, who has looked after both her parents in their old age as well as her mother-in-law. Indeed, she wrote a book about her experiences called *An Extra Pair of Hands*. She became an expert at finding little bits of time for herself and her husband: 'Greg and I have had caring responsibilities for a long time, so we are terribly good at looking at each other, going: "Quick pub lunch?" and zipping off whenever we can.'

Keeping friends and wider family in the loop about an elderly parent can be just one more thing to do on your long list, so consider having a WhatsApp group to manage this, posting a general message about Mum or Dad every now and then to update people.

Don't be afraid to lower your standards. Sometimes, looking after two generations can feel as if you're juggling, and if a ball drops, disaster will follow. But you can't pay attention to everyone at once, so focus on what's possible, not what you would like to do in a perfect world. The world isn't perfect, so try not to worry if you fall below your own high standards in caring for loved ones.

Be sure that you are claiming everything that you're entitled to, in terms of social welfare payments, and take advantage of any respite care that you're offered. Enlist the help of the wider family in order to get a well-earned break, and farm out tasks like cleaning to willing relatives or a cleaner if you can afford one. Even if it's just a one-off deep clean, it'll make you feel so much better. And remember, many organisations have support groups, where you can share the burden and a cup of tea with people in your situation. Counselling can also help, and Family Carers Ireland offers free counselling to carers – https://familycarers.ie/carer-supports/help-guidance/counselling.

6.

Looking Good and Feeling Great

'Style is something each of us already has.
All we need to do is find it.'

Diane von Furstenberg

Every now and again, something seismic happens that changes fashion in a fundamental way. After World War I, women went mad for dressing up in flapper dresses and wearing their hair short; after World War II, people began to opt for more casual, youth-oriented styles, and the teenager came into being. In this century, Covid-19 really affected style and fashion, and many of the things we wore 'BC' we no longer wear. For example, I recently went on the Brendan O'Connor show on RTÉ Radio 1 and, for some reason, thought I'd better wear a tie. Well, I nearly choked! It had been so long since I'd worn one, it felt very constricting. Nowadays, I'm inclined to dress smartly, but more casually, as I think many of us are. Some things really do change fashion and style for ever.

Having said that, the great thing about getting older is that I don't feel as self-conscious about my appearance, or as judgemental about others'! I happened to look back recently at my first book, *It's the Little Things*, and in particular at the chapter on style. I had to laugh out loud at my description of attending half-nine Mass in Kenmare and studying what people wore. I should have been praying, I know, but I couldn't help it! I used to give bonus points to people who dressed with particular style. 'An altar boy who wears the right shoes,' I proclaimed, 'gets two bonus points. And his mother gets more than two bonus points for making him wear proper shoes, because they look so much better under the soutane than a great big pair of trainers.' Bonus points were also awarded for washed hair and non-baggy jackets, wearing pyjamas indoors only and nothing to be worn back to front. It must have been the style back in 2014!

This does remind me of a funny story, however. When I went to Mass in Kenmare years ago, I'd keep an eye out for evidence of resourcefulness on the part of any of the altar boys. If I spotted any quick thinking on the altar, I'd think, *I'll give him a job.* (There were no altar girls at the time, just to be clear!) On this occasion, it was Midnight Mass on Christmas Eve – when Mass actually was at midnight – and as you can imagine, the church was packed to the rafters. It was very stuffy, with the crowds and the candles burning and so on. Because of the occasion, the priest processed up the middle aisle to the altar, followed by every altar boy from Kenmare to the Healy Pass, all looking very solemn, in rows of two. One of them was a boy called Anthony Palmer. Remember that name! As they got close to the altar, one of the boys suddenly leaned forward and collapsed onto the altar on his face with a huge crash. There was a sharp intake of breath and a deafening silence. Then Anthony turned around very quietly, grabbed the boy who'd fainted by the ankles and dragged him into the sacristy, like a dead body! He did the right thing, because the whole church was in hysterics laughing at him, so he needed to be got out of the way. I thought, *I'll give that boy a job when he turns 18.* I did, and he was brilliant. He worked with me for years!

I used to be a great man for the suits and needed everything to be just right. Nowadays, I dress more for myself and I enjoy it. I've downsized my suit collection considerably too. I want to feel comfortable, but also have a little bit of pizazz. I think that a lot of us fade into the background, style-wise, when we get older, but really, there's no need. Why not have fun and experiment a little, while being age-appropriate?

Contrary to what you might think from my 'bonus points' exercise, I'm not a big fan of rules about style and fashion for older people, because old age is the time when we can step away from rules and do our own thing. If we're no longer in the office, there's really no need for a suit, for men or women, unless you enjoy wearing one. Instead, you can experiment with softer shapes and even a bit of colour. However, I do like fashion journalist Jess Cartner-Morley's suggestion that we 'go 10 per cent more dressy for every ten years over 40'. She gives the example of jeans and a T-shirt, which can look fabulous when we're 25 but can make us blend into the furniture a little when we're older. Anyway, jeans are out for me: they don't fit me properly and I'd have to wear trainers with them – can you imagine?! If you do like jeans, make sure that they fit properly and don't hang off your rear! I prefer casual trousers that keep their shape well and don't crease. With that, I wear a collared shirt, not a T-shirt, because they can get baggy, and a sweater. I have quite the collection and I love bright colours – they really can suit older people. I think that colour can add definition and style to an older complexion.

Where Have All the Ties Gone?

I used to have the greatest collection of ties known to man, buying them on trips and ensuring I always had a matching pocket square in the breast pocket of my suit jacket. Only then did I feel I was fully dressed. However, I began to notice a creeping lack of ties whenever I watched men appearing on TV. They'd wear a suit with an open-necked shirt. At first, I was horrified, because they looked half-dressed. Then I discovered that in the fabled House of Commons men are no longer required to wear ties! As the BBC put it, 'they can loll about on the green benches as if they were at a family barbecue'. Apparently, according to the same piece by Brian Wheeler, if you turn up in an office wearing a tie nowadays, people will ask you if you have a court appearance!

From Oscar Wilde declaring that 'a well-tied tie is the first serious step in life' to Barack Obama at the G8 summit wearing an open-necked white shirt, it would seem the tie is no longer de rigueur. Whether they originated on the necks of Croatian soldiers in 1635 to keep them warm, or from the scraps of fabric attached to the clothes of Roman slaves to identify who owned them, ties became a staple of middle- and upper-class men's attire. In the era of factories and mills, if you wore a tie, you were part of the management class, because you knew it wasn't going get caught in the machinery. It makes sense, I suppose. A tie was always associated with membership of exclusive clubs, like golf clubs and gentlemen's clubs, and signalled that you were a cut above. Now, like the hat, which was always worn by men and women in public but began to disappear after World War II, the tie is going the same way. The rot set in, not with the House of Commons, but with the tech sector, which wanted to signal that they were too busy with ideas and forward thinking to bother dressing like 'suits'. When Mark Zuckerberg appears on TV, he does so in a plain black T-shirt and jeans – and it hasn't done him any harm. Covid seems to have driven the final nail into the necktie's coffin.

I must have been clairvoyant, because a few years ago I donated much of my collection to the local charity shop. I was very sad to lose some of my favourite Louis Feraud silk ties, but I knew that it was time to move on. Imagine my horror when I was driving up a country road a few weeks later and spotted a familiar-looking item holding the gate to a field full of cattle closed. You guessed: it was one of my designer ties! Some farmer clearly thought that was a good use for them ...

– Hair – What's Left of It! –

As we age, certain things happen to our hair. It can thin, or grow coarser, or break more easily. This is due to a combination of factors, from chlorine to the sun to chemicals in hair products. Stress can also play a part in hair loss, as can hormonal changes. Both men and women may find themselves losing hair, even though the reasons might be different. Many women complain about losing hair after childbirth and the menopause, when an increase in the male hormone androgen can cause the hair to thin. For men, the cause is usually genetic, but certain conditions, such as thyroid issues, can also contribute, in which case the loss might be accompanied by a rash or a damaged scalp.

When we get older, the growing phase of our hair becomes shorter and we produce less sebum, that natural oil that keeps your hair shiny, so you might find it becoming more brittle. Greyness is caused by a loss of melanin, that pigment that colours our hair, and we might also notice that our straight hair has become wavy and our curly hair is frizzy or even less curly. It's all a natural part of the ageing process. The latest research also indicates that digestive issues might play a part in hair loss, as might vitamin deficiencies.

The thing is that, for men and women, hair loss can be embarrassing and upsetting. Many people assume that women find the problem more disturbing, but men can find it hard, too. Having said that, I'd argue that hair loss is less socially acceptable for women, because people are simply less used to seeing it. If you are losing your hair, is there anything you can do about it? Yes, is the reassuring answer. So, before you reach for the specialist products (which can be expensive), try a few other things.

Washing your hair less frequently is a good place to start. You might have notice that, due to the reduction in sebum, it needs less washing anyway. Use a good conditioner, because your dry locks will benefit from it, and try a 'volumiser', which is a product that plumps up strands of hair to make them look thicker. Try to avoid things like straighteners, hairdryers and other styling devices that will dry your hair out. Another thing to try is to improve your diet. It certainly won't do any harm, and there is evidence that a diet higher in protein can help. Red meat (there's no harm once or twice a week), green leafy veg, eggs and avocados are all good. Check the levels of iron in your blood, too, as that can have an effect.

Some people have reported success using lavender oil to massage into their scalp. You'll certainly smell good! There's no real evidence for this treatment, but it won't do you any harm, provided you don't apply it neat – anything strong, no matter how natural, can give you a rash. Dilute it in another oil, like coconut or almond.

If the natural approaches aren't working for you, do go and see your doctor. For example, if you've had a stressful period in your life, it might well be the cause of your hair loss. Or the aforementioned pesky hormones, or indeed your medications. In that case, your GP will take a history to determine what might lie behind your hair thinning and, if necessary, pre-scribe treatments that may help you. The downside is they can be expensive and they don't always work. But sometimes a combination of things will work, such as a prescription shampoo, a protein-rich diet and stress reduction. You won't know until you chat to your GP and see what treatments might suit you. I am aware that certain people go on 'holiday' and come back with a fuller head of hair, but I'd be in no position to recommend it, even if I can understand how upsetting hair loss can be.

However, as a man with a head of white hair, I think that the decision about whether or not to go grey/silver/white is much easier for us men than for women. For a start, men's hair colour can look a peculiar shade if the dye is not applied properly, and society seems to accept grey-haired men more readily than women. But a lot has changed since the days of Just for Men, and if you don't like your grey, you can get it coloured. I'd definitely opt for a salon to start with, so that you can discuss what would suit your skin tone – very important. As we age, that really does change, so professional advice is just the ticket.

If you do opt to dye your hair at home, gentlemen, and you're only disguising a few greys, you can buy a specific product that will touch them up but won't give you a solid, dark colour that'll make you look like an alien! I know that there's a trend now for bleached blond hair, or even bright pastel colours, but I'd definitely go to a salon for this, as it's hard work to achieve that vivid look at home, should you lose the run of yourself! I would also stick to colours that are either a shade lighter or darker than your natural hair, so that you don't have that wine-coloured sheen that I sometimes see on TV.

If your hair is white, like mine, I'd be inclined to leave well alone, because the contrast between any colour dye and your natural hair will be too great. Thankfully, with the arrival of purple shampoo, getting rid of tricky yellow highlights in white hair is easy. Just don't use it too often or you'll get a blue rinse! I like American TV journalist Anderson Cooper's bright white hair – it looks smart and age-appropriate. I also like his style, which is short at the sides and long on top, combed to the side, but this is probably best if you have a good head of hair.

As to suitable hairstyles for older men, the days of

the comb-over are long gone, but I miss the sight of the long locks flying up in the wind! Nowadays, you can shave it tightly to your head so that you don't look 'bald' and I like that look. If you have strong features, you can even shave your head completely, like Dwayne 'The Rock' Johnson, but I'm always a bit puzzled by the vogue for a shaved head and a full beard: it makes me feel as if the person is upside down! If you are closely shaven on top, repeat it in your beard so that it looks tidy.

Of course, you don't have to shave your head if your hair is thinning – depending on where, of course. I always feel it's best not to try too hard to disguise a bald patch, because it'll look like exactly that. If your hairline is receding, however, don't comb it back – go forward. But use a product that'll give it texture and break it up, so you'll avoid the helmet look. A very tight, short back and sides, with the sides swept up a little, can draw the eye away from any bald patch. The current fashion for a 'skin fade' is basically a short back and sides, times two. The cut is 'faded' up from very tight at the neck and around the ears to longer on the top. How long depends on your hair. Go easy, though – some people have very elaborate fades over the ears, and you don't want topiary!

I would avoid dyeing your beard to match your hair, because it can look unnatural – most men's beards don't match their hair colour in real life. And speaking of beards ... there's been a trend for these giant Methuselah beards recently, that practically reach down to your feet! I'm not a fan, because they can look as if you've recently been on a desert island. Beards need as much care as hair, with regular trimming, tidying and using a product such as a beard oil to keep them healthy. I asked a few of the male staff in the hotel for tips and they tell me that washing it with a cleanser or beard shampoo is essential, as is combing it regularly to keep it tidy and in shape. A moisturiser is also important, I'm told – one that is suitable for your skin type – so your skin doesn't get red and flaky under the beard. I try to encourage the staff not to grow one in the high season in the hotel, because it can look very scruffy for the first while – and because they have to cover it in the kitchen with a kind of beard hammock!

For women, the question of colour is more complex. It's associated so much with youth that it can be hard to let go of the hair dye and embrace your greys. A friend of mine began to go grey in her 20s, and while it didn't bother her initially, when her own colour began to dull, she found that hair colour was her friend. However, she didn't try to maintain her former mid-brown, because the results looked harsh and unnatural. Instead, she opted for a light brown/ dark blonde. There's a reason paler colours suit older women: their skin tone. If your hair was black in your youth, I'd opt for something softer.

If you do decide to embrace the grey, remember that you can still get some nice silver highlights in it to lift the flatness, or indeed floodlights, a new technique that gives a subtler result (so I'm told). Either way, be sure to condition it regularly, as colour does damage the hair. And as to when to go grey, well, it depends. A few of my friends used lockdown to grow their colour out and were delighted with the natural results – and with the reduced bills at the hairdressers'!

If you want to grow your colour out, ultimately, it really is a case of just waiting it out, but you have a few options to soften the process. Talk to your hairdresser first and get some advice. Many will suggest that you let your hair grow out a little before visiting, so they can see what lies beneath! Some might suggest blending in some highlights or floodlights to soften that line between dyed and natural colour while it grows out. You could opt for a shorter hairstyle to help things along and, if you haven't bleached it, you can 'strip' the dye out, revealing your natural colour beneath. If you have bleached it, stripping won't work, unfortunately, so cold turkey might be your best option. Either way, grey or white hair is part and parcel of growing older, and I try to embrace it. I'm no longer trying to pretend that I'm a young fellow, and there's a great comfort in that. I can be exactly who I am!

– Shapes and Fit for Older Folk –

I'm a big fan of wearing whatever you like in old age: let the youngsters follow the rules! However, have you ever tried on something that you wore a year or two ago and it doesn't fit? This isn't necessarily because you've put on weight, but simply because your shape has changed. For example, I've lost quite a lot of weight, so I have to be careful that my clothes don't hang off me. Some people have put on weight in different places and find that their waistband is too tight or that their clothes pinch under the arms. Some men find that their derrière, to put it politely, has vanished and their trousers sag! That's the reality of getting older. The problem is that the fashion business isn't really aimed at the older dresser: women find that they are herded towards drab colours and sensible jackets and men are encouraged to fade to beige and navy. So what can we do to look our best and, more importantly, have fun?

When it comes to style for both men and women in this age group, it really is about fit. And this means looking at the body shape you have now – not the one you had 20 years ago – and dressing for that shape. A woman friend of mine tells me that she used to buy clothes that were a size or two too small for her, with the aim of fitting into them after the diet, but now she accepts that she's an older woman, healthy and well, and dresses for who she is. She's petite, with a waist, so finds that A-line dresses work for her, that emphasise her waist, but don't draw attention to other areas – I'm just passing this on! She also finds that tunic dresses that stop at the knee skim over the things she doesn't want to draw attention to, but don't make her look short or like she's wearing a tent. However, she did say that if you're petite and light in frame, something that defines you, like properly fitting jeans and a short blazer, is a good look. If you're little, slouchy or over-sized is not your friend, and nor are vivid patterns, which can drown you.

If you're tall and thin, you might look great in a well-cut jacket and a pair of trousers that stop at the ankle and have a bit of definition at the waist. You don't have to look like someone from *Star Trek*, however, all angles! You can opt for a softer suit with a crisp white shirt, but use a belt. It will hold up your trousers (always a good thing!) and give your waist that definition.

I have been doing my homework, you'll be glad to know, and came across an interesting video by an older woman, Tricia Cusden, with lots of advice on body shape and clothing. She advises that, if you're heavier on the bottom, opt for simple trousers and keep the attention on your top half with a bright jacket, scarf or statement jewellery. On the other hand, if you are larger on top, draw the attention away from, say, your shoulders, by wearing a simple tailored jacket on top and trousers, both of which define you without being frumpy.

Many women tell me that they aren't sure about leggings once they get to a certain age, but with so many modern fabrics on the market and such comfort, you can wear them and still look good. The key is to buy the best quality that you can afford, so that they won't bag around the knees. And you don't need to buy spray-on leggings either. Some retailers have leggings that are looser from the knee down, so they're more flattering, more like jeans really. High-waisted leggings also offer more comfort. Whatever you decide to wear, a longer tunic top looks more flattering with leggings. Jeggings are basically leggings that resemble skinny jeans and can look very chic with a knit or long cardigan and tunic top.

Don't kill the messenger here – a friend told me that unless you are very slender, try not to wear tight clothing. That doesn't mean you have to wear huge kaftans, like Demis Roussos! It really is about comfort and feeling at ease in what you're wearing, not that the seams are cutting into you. Instead, opt for simple cuts that drape to cover any lumps and bumps, rather than those that pinch. Wraparound tops can be good, because they can be adjusted and they add definition. And don't forget chic hairstyles – we can go a lot softer now that a shampoo and set isn't de rigueur – so, don't settle for a frumpy look from your hairstylist. Your hair and body shape might have changed, but you aren't destined to look forever older because of it.

Women can wear great accessories nowadays and have fun with them. I love what Prue Leith wears – she's a cookery expert and is on the *Great British Bake Off*. She goes for bright shades and chunky jewellery and it really suits her, because she's tall. If you feel shy about experimenting, aim for one piece of jewellery or a bright scarf or a bold pair of glasses to give definition to your face. Smaller people might find that chunky jewellery 'wears' them, but why not experiment? Instead of a necklace made up of lots of chunky pieces, you could wear one with just one – a stone in a bright colour, for example.

I think that adopting a new look can give you great confidence. You feel like a bolder, brighter you, and I'd recommend it. If you're unsure what looks good on you, many department stores offer personal shopping services and will help you – and you don't have to buy! Make it clear that you're just trying a new look. As a friend of mine says every time I moan about fashion for older people, 'Well, nobody's looking at you!' It makes me laugh and she has a point. The focus of attention is on the younger generation, but this can be very liberating. Ultimately, you can do and wear what you like!

If you are looking for a few quick tips on style for older women, here are my favourites:

- Wear natural fabrics: cotton, linen, wool. They look so much better on more mature folk.
- Opt for bold colours, because they can really lift an older complexion, but be wary of patterns.
- Black can look a bit harsh on us oldies: if you want to buy a blazer, try navy or grey instead.
- Some style gurus say no to leather jackets, but I think that a simple, well-cut leather (or faux leather) jacket without embellishments can look very stylish. Maybe ditch the rhinestones and fringing, though!
- Capri pants don't really flatter when you're older, because they cut you off in the wrong place, and they can look baggy at the knees. But well-cut dark-blue jeans can look very smart and can be dressed up or down as needed.
- Cardigans are undoubtedly comfortable, and for those of us with the proverbial 'bingo wings' (I say this to men and women, by the way!) they can be a godsend. They're also just the ticket for the Irish weather. I'd opt for tidy rather than baggy styles, however, so they don't drown you, and wear them unbuttoned.
- Sleeves. A friend of mine once produced a garment that looked like one leg of a legging, with a hole in the middle. This, she informed me, was 'sleeves'

– basically, a pair of cardigan sleeves joined by a minute bit of fabric at the back. I could see the point, I suppose ... Plenty of women feel self-conscious about their arms when they get older, they tell me, preferring to wear three-quarter-length sleeves. Others wear sleeveless tunic dresses with a cardigan thrown over the top. I say, wear whatever you feel like wearing! If you're not bothered, so what? The above are merely suggestions.

– Style for Men –

I feel that I'm on firmer ground here, because I've adapted and changed my look as the years have gone by and I have got a good idea what works for me. Some of us men can be shy about fashion and feel that it's not for us, but I'd argue that it is, even if the goal is just to look smart and presentable. You don't have to go for mustard and navy, baggy jumpers or ill-fitting trousers.

The first item on the agenda for so many of us older men is where to put the belt if we now have a bit of a tummy. Do we lift it above our bellies and wear it under our armpits? No! But wearing it under our bellies isn't a good look either, because it all hangs over the belt. The ideal place to wear a belt is on your bellybutton. 'But hang on,' I hear you say ... I'd argue that if you are in possession of a bit of a tummy, there's no point in wishing it away. Just accept it and adapt accordingly. You'll find that your trousers sit better where they were intended to sit, even if you have extra padding.

But first, get trousers and jeans that fit properly. Go to a retailer and ask for advice. Yes, it might be embarrassing, but they'll have seen all sorts, and they will know what works for different body shapes. High-rise jeans and trousers work better if you have a tummy, and a jacket works wonders to give you a bit of streamlining. Layering can often be a great idea: a T-shirt worn with an open shirt and a jacket can narrow your silhouette. And, while it might sound counter-intuitive, baggy clothes will actually draw attention to the bits you want to hide, so keep them comfortable, not too loose and not too tight. Just as it is for women of a certain age, the correct fit comes before any other consideration.

Slogan T-shirts might be amusing when you're 20, but when you get to 50, it might be time to tuck them away. I think they can make us look as if we're trying too hard. And while I've never really been a T-shirt man, the style gurus suggest that we steer clear of V-neck T-shirts that draw the eye to our tummies and to the sprouting of grey hairs on our chests. I met a man at a barbecue who was wearing such a T-shirt and, quite honestly, my eyes kept straying to that V-neck! Confidence at an older age is all about simplicity and wearing it well.

I've noticed that there's a fashion among younger men for wearing shorts in winter. Why on earth you'd do that is beyond me, but my shorts-wearing days are over, I can assure you! And if you're like me, shorts will reveal your skinny legs ... Of course, they're fine on holiday, but for daily wear I think that jeans or chinos look smarter, with a flat front, which is more flattering. And while younger men might be able to 'rock' a pair of skinny jeans, I'm not convinced that it's for the over 50s ... Again, it's about fit – and wearing clothing that's too tight will be uncomfortable.

If you're a fan of colour, stick to a bright jumper or scarf or T-shirt under a jacket. No wine cords worn with a bright-yellow shirt and a mustard jacket! Daniel Craig can get away with wearing a bright-pink velvet jacket to the premiere of *No Time to Die*, but he sensibly kept the rest of his outfit plain to make it really pop.

I was highly entertained recently when I came across the Rounderbum men's butt-enhancing padded trunks, which is basically underwear with padding to give you a behind! I laughed out loud, but they are addressing a significant problem among us older folk: the flat behind. I'm not sure that I would go quite so far as to buy padded underwear, because I believe in working with what you have, but I would try to

buy trousers in good fabrics that don't sag or cling.
If you're a woman, emphasising your waist – say, in
a dress with a fitted waist and an A-line skirt – can
draw attention away from a 'pancake' behind. If you're
a man, a correctly fitting jacket or a sweater worn
above your behind will not advertise its flatness.

A Note about Shapewear

Did you know that shapewear first appeared around
1600 BC? Who knew! Apparently, the Ancient Greeks
had a penchant for emphasising all their best bits,
but, interestingly, they weren't bothered about their
waists. By contrast, the Romans wanted flat chests and
rounded hips and wore binders and padding accordingly. The 'hourglass' shape that we recognise today in
women's fashion really came into its own in the Middle
Ages, when the corset came into being. No matter what
size you were, you tightened it to the point that you
could no longer breathe properly. Can you imagine?!
The Victorians weren't any better: corsets were made of
whalebone and were fitted so tightly that you'd have to
lie down on the floor and get your friend/maid to tie it
for you. Now, with advances in technology, shapewear
is thankfully more comfortable, but the idea of the
'perfect' silhouette persists. A certain Kardashian has
her own line of shapewear with tiny waists and large
derrières, and now men can avail of T-shirts and briefs

that cinch them in all the right places. The fashion editor of male style magazine *GQ* decided to give an ultra-sculpt T-shirt a go and reported: 'My main fear as I settled in for *GQ*'s Monday morning meeting was that my stomach might pop through the fabric, like a herniated intestine'! What a lovely thought.

– Shoes Maketh the Man and Woman –

A lot of us, men and women, struggle with shoes at this stage. I have a wonky foot, but I've had that since birth, so I need to have my shoes specially made by a lovely family firm called Tuttys in Kildare. For casual wear, a lot of older people opt for a trainer/walking-shoe hybrid for maximum comfort. This is great for walking the dog, and there are lots of much trendier styles out there for us, thankfully. A few tips for older people include:

- Opt for shoes with removable insoles, for those of us who need to wear orthotics.
- Look for a secure, high back to stabilise your ankle: a friend of mine took a walk one day in shoes with a low back and the lack of stability caused her to fall and break her ankle – she now refers to them as the 'shoes of doom'!
- Lucky is the woman who can wear very high heels at an older age, because our feet are simply less

flexible. Instead, try a wedge heel, or a platform (with ankle support), or a kitten heel with a dress.

- If you want a dressier shoe but don't fancy a heel, a loafer can be nice, because it's wider at the toes and a bit more supportive than, say, a flat shoe. The trend for ankle boots is also continuing, and these offer comfort and support as well as being fashion-forward. You can afford to be dressier in your shoe choices when you get a bit older.
- As a rule of thumb, I'd suggest avoiding trainer shops – leave them to the youngsters! – and instead go for trendy but age-appropriate trainers that don't have garish logos or big thick soles, or, Heaven forfend, are white! Keep it simple and stylish, and avoid glitter or leopard print, or both! Simple block colours can look trendy and fun, but suitable to our age group.

– *Accessorise* ... –

I recently came across the Instagram account of Iris Apfel, the New York fashion icon. She's the older lady who wears giant black round-rimmed glasses and wonderful accessories. Her slogan is 'more is more and less is a bore'. She breaks every single fashion 'rule' and looks fantastic. Clashing colours, patterns, bows, giant jewellery pieces ... she wears them all and with such style. We can't all be her, but we can learn that bold accessories and statement jewellery can really make an impact. But she does stick to bright, simple clothing shapes and makes them pop with huge necklaces and wonderful glasses.

Contrary to my advice about wearing age-appropriate clothing, wearing a trendy pair of glasses is a great idea. There's nothing that dates you quite like your glasses! And glasses add definition to your face and a certain boldness to your appearance. Keep the shape simple, though – no wings or other things hanging off them! And the current trend for 1980s-style gold-rimmed specs is for the youngsters. They will still make the rest of us look like John Major … Jeff Goldblum is an older American actor who looks fantastic in his heavy black-framed glasses.

If you like bags, opt for simple shapes and classic styles that are well made. Irish men have a thing about bags, I'd argue, but I think they can be very practical, as well as smart. A shoulder bag in a simple shape and quality fabric can be a great place for the newspaper, phone and keys. Better than your trouser pockets, anyway – or, worse, the bag for life (you know who you are …). And the bonus is your hands are free, should you need them for a walking cane. Italian men wear great 'man bags', and they make absolute sense.

Women are allowed to have more fun with bags, I think, but I'd still opt for well made at this stage, rather than fashionable. For example, 'dumpling' bags are a trend at the time of writing: they are soft and resemble a dumpling in the way that they've been pinched in at the top. If you want to catch that trend, by all means buy one, but don't spend a fortune on it, as trends pass. A female friend of mine jokes about cross-body bags being a mark of old age, but they are practical! If you want one, why not buy one? Older arms are not meant for giant bucket bags with tassels hanging off them. But go for one that looks smart – you can opt for a pop of colour, too.

A friend of mine who is petite tries to avoid large tote bags, because she says they make her look like a bag with legs! I never noticed, but if you're on the smaller side, go for something neater; if you're taller, a teensy-weensy handbag might look a bit out of proportion, but the large tote might be just the ticket.

When it comes to scarves, I'm deferring to my female friends again! Recently, people have been going around with blankets wrapped around them, and this certainly looks cosy, but it can drown us older folk. I was highly entertained, however, when I Googled some scarf ideas and was directed to 'old lady scarves', whatever they are! I have no intention of insulting my older friends here, so let's bypass them.

Many older women have taken on board the message that a scarf can really finish an outfit, and that's great, but again I'd steer away from busy prints to avoid looking as if the scarf is wearing you. Why not wear your prints on your lower half and keep the top half for block colours, including your scarf? If you are fond of a pattern, try a smaller one. Also, try not to wear a scarf that's too big, wrapped around your neck like a boa constrictor! Aim for scarves that will go with a number of outfits, and try not to buy a scarf just because it looks lovely. A friend of mine loves Paris, and when she discovered a silk scarf with a map of her favourite city on it, she jumped at it. What could be more romantic, she thought? It turns out that wearing a very large map of a city around her neck didn't work at all! So, now her scarf hangs on the wall in her living room, and she can wander the streets of Paris to her heart's content. However, the same friend tells me that a scarf can be a really good way to 'break' the colour of your top, if it's in a colour that you love but doesn't quite work for you. Great advice!

When it comes to men, many of them are squeamish about wearing a scarf, unless it has a rugby or football logo on it! However, I'm a big fan of a simple scarf in a plain colour that works with my knitwear, and I can't see why it wouldn't work for most men. Bold patterns or novelty prints are not our friend, but colour can most definitely be, as can quality fabrics. A bright-red scarf worn with a grey jumper can really lift it, for example. I did like the advice on www.realmenrealstyle.com, however, which told me that there were various 'manly' ways to tie a scarf ... I had no idea! I simply wrap one around my neck and let the two ends hang down and that's it. However, if you'd like to get fancy about it, you can opt for a jaunty Parisian knot, which involves folding your scarf in half to make a loop and putting the ends through that loop, tying it at the side. It does indeed look French and quite smart! However, I'm no fan of flicking the ends over my shoulder, Dr Who style, or of simply wearing it draped around my neck or shoved into the font of my suit. My whole self screams 'No'! Less is most definitely more when it comes to men wearing a scarf.

And, while I'm on the subject of accessories, I was in London recently at a conference of Master Innholders, 600 of the country's top hoteliers, and I found myself retelling an old story about a cummerbund. I'm not sure if young men wear them any more, but they were a brightly coloured silk sash, which you wore around your middle to match your bow tie in a dress suit.

Now, every New Year's Eve in the 1980s, we'd have a big party at the Park Hotel Kenmare. The ladies would dress up to the nines in designer clothing and they'd make their grand entrance down the staircase. I'd always try to dress my suit up to join in the fun. I was in Paris in my favourite shop, Louis Feraud – of the silk ties – and I bought a matador jacket. This was a short jacket just like a matador would wear (it *was* the 1980s!). It was beautiful – silver and maroon – and I loved it, but of course, because of its length, my shirt would be sticking out at the back, so I thought, *I need a cummerbund*. Now, Dunnes Stores and M&S did sell them, but with an elasticated back, so they would only cover the front of your outfit. I wanted a cummerbund that went all the way round my waist. And do you think I could find one? Not in the entire city of Dublin.

A few days later, I was in London for a Small Luxury Hotels meeting and I thought I'd go down to Savile Row and have a look there. I was in a hurry to get a midday flight, so I rushed down at 8.55 in the morning, and the first shop I went into was Gieves & Hawkes. The minute I set foot in the place, I immediately thought, *I shouldn't be here*. Everything was displayed in a glass case, and if you wanted a tie, they'd open the case and show it to you. Before I could turn around and leave, this gentleman appeared and said, 'Good morning, sir, can I help you?'

'I am looking for a proper cummerbund,' I said.

'Oh my goodness, I haven't sold anyone a cummerbund for 30 years,' he said, before shouting, 'George?' Next thing, a man called George steps out of the shadows and my friend says, 'This gentleman is looking for a cummerbund. You could try Militia.'

'Oh, yes,' George said, smiling at me. Then he said, 'I'll show you a shortcut.' So off we went, down one set of stairs and up another, until we arrived on the first floor. A gentleman was sitting at a big round desk with a huge ledger open in front of him. Beside him was a very large American man in a ten-gallon hat and his wife. The conversation went like this.

The shop assistant says to him: 'Double breasted?'

Ten Gallon says to his wife: 'Double breasted?'

His wife nods to the assistant: 'Double breasted.'

Shop assistant: 'Standard lapels?'

Ten Gallon to his wife: 'Standard lapels?'

Wife to assistant: 'Standard lapels.'

'Covered buttons ... inside leg ...?' And so it went on through all the possible permutations. Meanwhile, I was looking at the glass cases, which seemed to contain uniforms of various kinds, and then I see a Beefeater jacket and an army dress jacket. The penny dropped. I thought, *Oh Sacred Heart, thank God that man was occupied when I arrived*, because I wanted to speak to Militia – I thought it was a woman! I had no idea that 'Militia' was the military department. My heart was pumping, an Irishman in the wrong place.

Eventually, the assistant closed the big ledger and turned to me. 'I'm terribly sorry for the delay. How can I help you?'

'I'm looking for a cummerbund,' I said.

'Oh, goodness me, I haven't been asked for one ...'

'I know, but I hoped you might have one. I need it for a particular jacket, to go all the way around,' I explained, miming the shape of my lovely matador jacket.

'I see,' he said. He opened a dusty wooden drawer and started rooting through a collection of military badges and pins. 'No, nothing there,' he said. He opened another drawer that contained epaulettes and ties for a dress uniform, then a third. 'Hold on a moment, you might be in luck,' he said, taking out an ancient plastic bag and putting it on the counter. It was indeed a cummerbund. He started unwinding it – three feet, then six feet, then nine feet – he was almost out the window unravelling this cummerbund! I thought, *Do you buy it by the yard? And if you do, I bet it's £200 a yard in Gieves & Hawkes.*

I summoned up the courage. 'May I ask how much it is?'

He picked up the ancient label affixed to the cummerbund with a piece of string and a pin. 'Oh, I need my glasses,' he said, putting them on and peering at the label. 'Oh, it's in the old money!' So he got a calculator, pressed a few buttons and announced, 'It's £2.'

A mere £2 for 40 yards of cummerbund! I took it and I came home and spent the next week trying to work out how to put it on and secure it. I ended up wrapping it around myself 15 times, but then wondered where on earth the flap went. Eventually, I tucked it in and pinned it, and it more or less held up for the night.

7.

Finances for Older People

'A wise person should have money in their heart
and not in their head.'

Jonathan Swift

I know the price of everything. Even today, I can tell you that butter has gone from €2.17 to €3.39 in one supermarket! What is the cow doing that she didn't do before, I wonder? I can't work it out. Anyway, this is by way of introduction to a little story about myself as a younger man. I was working in Jurys Hotel in Ballsbridge at the time, and Peter Malone was the general manager. He was a very nice man, but he liked to keep staff on their toes.

Quite often, he'd ring down from his office with a question designed to catch us out. All the juniors used to say, 'Ehm, uhm, I'll ring you back,' and hope that he'd forget!

At this time, I was in cost control, and he rang down and said, 'Brennan, what's the price of salmon?'

Of course, being a grocer's son, I shot back, 'Fresh, smoked or organic?'

There was a long silence, so I think I'd caught *him* out. Eventually, he answered, 'All three.'

'Fresh is £1.79 a pound, smoked is £5.99 a pack and organic is €1.90,' I said.

'Oh.'

'That's this morning's prices, Mr Malone,' I added. And he hung up!

Because of Dad, I know prices – that's just the way I am. Also, after a lifetime in business, I've become comfortable with the concept of money. However, in my working life, 'money' is really all about figures on a balance sheet, some not as large as I'd like! I've got used to scanning spreadsheets and understanding things like capital balances and profit-and-loss calculations. I suppose I'm good with business money. However, when it comes to personal finance, I'm probably as clued in as everyone else of my age – i.e. it varies! According to Age Action, who campaign for better financial services for older people, 11 per cent of people don't use the internet at all. In fact, according to European statistics, only 40 per cent of the elderly in Ireland use the internet. You can imagine what that means for those who are trying to navigate the confusing world of online banking.

Recently, my friend Aisling helped her mother to pay a credit card bill online with her bank – which shall be nameless! Her mother is a whizz with all things online, but this bank required her to complete no fewer than ten steps, involving two separate devices, a laptop and a card reader, to pay the €19.56 she owed. Is it any wonder us oldies don't feel confident about online banking? Not only that, but there are obvious security risks to having to ask someone to help you with online banking – probably the very risks the banks are trying to avoid, to be fair to them.

Online banking can present a challenge to those of us who are older, not least because of the issue of fraud. But before I give you a fright, I'd like to share some positive tips to help you with your finances as you age. I've also spoken to Susan Hayes Culleton, a financial expert, who not only answered my questions but also provided a lot of additional information about finances and the elderly. You'll see this in my chat with Susan at the end of this chapter. Thanks to her, I now feel much better equipped than I was!

If you've read Chapter 1, you'll know that planning is important when it comes to retirement. I came across this quote from actor Michael Caine – no slouch when it comes to investing his money – that said, 'Save your money. You're going to need twice as much money in your old age as you think.' My answer to him would be, 'That depends!' Those of us who haven't been fortunate enough in life to make a ton of money – and that's most of us – will quake at the very idea of needing 'twice as much', but is that really true?

According to the Pension Support Line – www.pensionsupportline.ie – you'll need roughly 50 per cent of your gross pre-retirement income to live comfortably. So, if you earned €40,000 a year, €20,000 is what you'll need. Remember, the state pension is currently €13,172 per annum, so there might well be a shortfall. If you'd like to calculate exactly what your needs might be, my financial whizz Susan Hayes Culleton has directed me to the following: https://www.pensionsauthority.ie/en/lifecycle/useful-resources/pension-calculator/. Another useful tool is www.misc.ie/home. This is a minimum income spending calculator that allows you to work out the minimum income on which you could manage, given your lifestyle.

One thing to remember is that your mortgage, if applicable, will probably have been paid off, and your children will be reared, please God, so your outgoings won't be what they were. But of course you'll probably have greater need of health insurance, if you have it, and that can be expensive.

The good news is that you can apply for health insurance at any time: companies are not allowed to exclude you on the grounds of your age. However, they are allowed to apply 'loading' of 2 per cent per annum to people over the age of 34. So, if you take out health insurance at 30, and it costs €2,000 per year, at 34, it'll cost you 8 per cent more, that is, €2,160. The Health Insurance Authority is the place to go for advice: www.hia.ie.

If you don't have private health insurance, you can, of course, avail of the public health system. The care is the same – the only issue, as some of you will know, is waiting times, which have been affected by Covid. You will know about the emergency department charges of €100 for those without a medical card – if you have a medical card, you won't be charged to go to A&E, and since April 2023 the €80 per night hospital-stay fee is no more, so that's good news. For those who don't have a medical card, the GP visit card caters for children of six and under, as well as the under-70s, subject to a means test. However, you can have a higher income and still qualify for a GP visit card. Those of you who are over 70 can visit your GP for free, and the government is currently looking at expanding the scheme – www.citizensinformation.ie will tell you all you need to know about medical cards and GP visit cards.

If you don't have health insurance but want to opt for private care – for example, if there's a lengthy waiting list for treatment – you can certainly do so, but you will pay for the full cost of the procedure and relevant tests. If you take out health insurance, then are promptly diagnosed with a condition, most insurers will apply a 26-week waiting period before you can claim. Once you have a 'pre-existing' condition – that is, an illness you had before taking out health insurance – the waiting time, according to the Health Insurance Authority, is five years. It pays to have a good think about it and talk to your GP, who will advise you on the best course of action. You can also call the payments department of the relevant private hospital for further information on costs. They will provide you with details of the costs and any payment plans they might have – but, again, discuss your options with your GP.

The other thing to remember is that if you are still working you can offset medical expenses against your taxes – indeed, you can offset medical expenses that might not be yours, but which you've paid for.

Say you've paid for orthodontic treatment or doctors' appointments for your children – well, you can claim them also at the rate of tax that you pay. Good to know!

– Working in Retirement –

With many of us living to a ripe old age nowadays, there's nothing to stop us working during our retirement. Yes, really! But before you get too excited, if you've worked in the public sector before retirement and return to work in that sector, your pension might be affected. However, if you opt to work in the private sector, this isn't the case. If you were employed in the private sector, you can return to work and might even be able to continue to pay pension contributions to boot – but you'll need to check what your pension scheme, if you have one, allows.

If you are in receipt of social welfare benefits, you can do a certain amount of work and receive some of your Jobseeker's Allowance. Check this and other employment matters with your local Intreo centre. Generally, you'll also continue to pay PRSI if you are working and are under the age of 66. However, according to Citizens Information, you can earn up to €352 per week without needing to pay PRSI – good news! Again, check the details with your local Intreo centre.

As regards tax, if you are over 65 and have an income of less than €18,000 per annum, you won't pay tax on that amount. If you're married or in a civil partnership that amount is €36,000. However, you may well be liable for PRSI (as mentioned above) and USC, and your pension and some social welfare benefits are taxable. Just so you know!

– Other Benefits –

Ever heard of the Living on a Specified Island payment? I hadn't, until I started researching the benefits that you can claim as an older person. It goes to show that there may be benefits out there for you that you don't know about. Now is the time to start looking into them – you might be surprised at what you're entitled to.

We've looked into the pension situation earlier – thank God! – so these payments are supplementary to that. Firstly, if you are a widow, widower or a surviving civil partner, you might be entitled to a pension, either 'contributory' – i.e. through your PRSI payments – or 'non-contributory', which will be means tested. The Living Alone Increase applies to those on social welfare payments who may be living alone. Now, perhaps you might think that you don't qualify if you're living in a granny flat attached to your family home, but if you have your own cooking or dining facilities, that counts as 'living alone'. Sheltered accommodation can be included also, but you'll need to check with the Department of Social Protection to see if your home is on their list. Nursing homes are not included, or shared accommodation, but if you have a relative or friend who stays overnight only, for example, you are still classed as 'living alone'. This lengthy link will tell you all you need to know: https://www.citizensinformation.ie/en/social_welfare/ social_welfare_payments/extra_social_welfare_ benefits/living_alone_allowance.html. The rate in 2022 was €22.00 per week.

You might also qualify for a fuel allowance, particularly if you are receiving social welfare benefits. It's worth €33 per week – and, of course, there were extra top-ups in 2022/3 due to the cost of fuel, which was good news for those with soaring bills. And hopefully, in the future, we'll be less reliant on fossil fuels. Did you know that Ireland produced a third of its electricity from wind in 2023? It makes sense, given our status as one of the windiest places in Europe. The other scheme to look at is the Household Benefits Package, which helps with fuel and the TV licence; it's not means tested if you're over 70, but if you're under 70 and on certain benefits, such as the social welfare allowance or the state pension, you may still qualify.

The Carer's Allowance is payable to those looking after someone who needs care because of age, illness or disability on a full-time basis. It is means tested, but if you are in receipt of a payment from the Department of Social Welfare, you can still qualify. And if you're earning and single, the first €350 of your gross weekly income is disregarded. If you're married, that rises to €750 per week. And, if your dependent goes into a nursing home, for example, you will receive the allowance for a further 12 weeks. Now, some of you might worry about receiving it if your loved one goes to a day centre, for example, but that's just fine – you'll still qualify, and they can also be in hospital for up to 13 weeks (adults, that is) without your allowance being affected. In 2022, the Carer's Allowance for someone over 66, caring for one other, was €262 per week. It is taxable, though. If in doubt, head for your local Intreo centre, where they will be able to tell you what your entitlements are.

And as for that Living on a Specified Island Allowance ... do you know, it makes complete sense! If you are living on one of the islands off the coast of Ireland, you'll encounter additional expenses – those of you who do are probably nodding your heads at me right now! So, there is an additional payment available to those aged over

66 in receipt of certain benefits – for example, a pension. Before you get too excited, there is a list of designated islands, from Aranmore in Donegal to Whiddy in Cork, but it's quite extensive: www.gov.ie/en/publication/371e50-operational-guidelines-increase-for-living-on-a-specified-island.

Finally, the Additional Needs Payment is a one-off payment to help people with sudden expenses such as car repairs or a new boiler, household furniture or travel expenses to hospital. It doesn't have a limit, as such, because of the nature of the payment, but you can apply through your local Intreo office, and the government have helpful examples of qualifying needs on this page: https://www.gov.ie/en/publication/47dd9-examples-of-applications-for-the-additional-needs-payment.

Staying Warm in the Winter

An older friend of mine opened an energy bill recently to find that gas and electricity had cost her €975! That's for two months' use for two elderly people. That might seem very high, but older people are generally more sensitive to the cold. Certain medications can make them feel colder, as can conditions like diabetes. Also, your skin thins as you age, making you more suscept-ible. It's a priority for older people to be warm and well, and according to advice from the HSE in this handy little leaflet – https://www.hse.ie/eng/services/

publications/olderpeople/wellandwarm.pdf – the temperature in your home should be 21 degrees Celsius if you're moving around and 24 degrees if you're sitting watching TV. That might seem high to younger people – it seems balmy to me! – but older folk are susceptible to hypothermia, so their environment needs to be warmer.

The HSE reminds us that eating a hot meal and drinking hot drinks can help to keep you warm – make sure to have a hot cuppa throughout the day and before bed. Your local Meals on Wheels service can drop in with a hot meal if you aren't able to make one – and don't forget that supermarkets will deliver to you if you can't get out.

Dress warmly, with layers rather than one bulky item, and heat up your bed and bedroom before you go to bed, so that you don't get a chill. If you find heating your entire home too expensive, heat your bedroom and living room as a priority. According to the HSE, this is better than inadequate heating of the whole house. If you are struggling to pay your bills, call your energy supplier and explain your situation. You can talk to them about payment plans and ask to be placed on their Special Services Register. This means that your fuel won't be cut off between November and March, which will come as a relief, I'm sure.

If you're older and need to upgrade your home to

make it more energy efficient, the Warmer Homes scheme might be able to help. This will cover things like attic insulation and draught-proofing. The number to call is 1800 250 204 to be placed in touch with local suppliers.

Living on a Limited Income

No matter how much you earned when you were working or how much you saved, your limited income in retirement could still come as a bit of a shock to you. Some of us will have benefitted from generous pension schemes or retirement plans, but for various reasons you might find that your finances are stretched. So how can older people manage their finances on a budget? Thankfully, there are two sources of great information on managing your money. The first is the Competition and Consumer Protection Commission – www.ccpc.ie. Along with consumer advice, they also give advice on how to budget, how to complete a financial health check to monitor your outgoings and incomings, how to set savings goals, whether it's for a holiday or for a one-off emergency, and so on. They have a specific area devoted to retirement finances, and it makes great sense: this includes thinking about investments and risk, how to use a pension lump sum – very important! – shopping around for better deals on insurance and releasing equity in your home (I'll get to that shortly). The other excellent resource is the Money Advice and Budgeting Service (MABS) – www.mabs.ie. They also have a helpline for those in financial crisis: 0818 07 2000.

Now, to the issue of equity release. This has been talked about quite a bit in the media, and the benefits seem obvious to many homeowners. You have a lot of money locked up in your home and you'd like to avail of it, say, to take the trip of a lifetime or to give a gift to your grandchildren. Great – but, in case you think it's too good to be true, equity release isn't free money! One form of equity release, a 'lifetime loan', is basically a mortgage that you take out against the value of your home, but the key difference is that you don't have to make regular repayments and the loan can be repaid upon your death or if you decide to sell. But (and there's always a but!) the interest rates on this type of loan are high – 6.45 per cent – and it gets added to the sum borrowed every month, accruing compound interest, which some of us will remember from school! So that can build up pretty quickly. I came across a very good article on the RTÉ website about the subject and noted that one financial consultant, Michael Dowling, calculated that 'in effect, the debt increases by 35 per cent every five years'. That's food for thought! You can opt to make regular repayments, however, on the interest, which means that the loan itself won't grow, and if you have a 'negative equity clause' in your home, that means that, unlike a regular mortgage, the only asset available to the lender is your home. However, while you might think that it won't be your problem in the end, remember, you'll be leaving less to your children. Of course, that's your choice, but many advisors suggest that you discuss it with them first to avoid any nasty shocks when you die.

I'm not here to lecture anyone on the dos and don'ts of this scheme, but what I would say is, do your homework on this and all of the options available to you, so that you know what the pros and cons are.

Again, the CCPC has detailed information on equity-release schemes. Here's what they suggest:

> If you are considering an equity-release scheme, get independent legal and financial first and consider the alternatives, including:
> - selling your home and moving to a cheaper or smaller one
> - getting a different type of mortgage if you have an income to meet the repayments
> - renting out one or more rooms
> - transferring ownership to a family member in return for the cash you need and the right to live in the property for life. Be sure to get

independent legal advice if you are con-
sidering this option. (https://www.ccpc.ie/
consumers/money/mortgages/equity-release)

In fact, the CCPC suggests that you seek legal advice
on any decisions you might make in this area, which
seems very sensible to me. They also refer to another
type of equity-release scheme that I thought you'd
like to know about: home reversion schemes. This
means, in essence, that a company will buy a share in
your home for a fixed lump sum. They will then own
a share in your home, which they will redeem when
the house is sold or if you leave it permanently – say,
to go into a home. Bingo, you might think, but as the
CCPC points out, the set-up fees can be expensive,
because your home will need to be independently
valued and so on, and, of course, the big issue is
that 'The money you receive will be much less than
the market value of the share in your property. The
difference between the market value and the lump
sum you receive for the share you sell is the true
cost of these schemes. If you don't live long, it may
prove very expensive.' If this seems complicated to
you, go to their page on the subject – linked above
– and look at the examples they provide to see just
what's involved. Also, if you avail of this option, look
into whether or not it will affect your eligibility for
the government's Fair Deal scheme, in which your

nursing-home fees are recouped from the value of your home when you die.

An Interview with the Positive _Economist, Susan Hayes Culleton_

Susan is the managing director of the Hayes Culleton Group. She is the author of five books, including *The Savvy Woman's Guide to Making Money* and *The Savvy Guide to Making More Money*. She hosts two YouTube shows, including *Savvy Investors at VectorVest*, is a regular keynote speaker and is a Chartered Financial Analyst charter-holder. I asked her a few questions on your behalf about money and older people, and she kindly gave me the benefit of her wisdom. I learned a lot!

Q: If you had to give one piece of advice to older people on managing their money, what would it be?

A: Can I give three? First, I don't assume that all of those 60 and over are wealthy, but according to the CSO, 'the median net wealth of households with one adult and children under 18 is €5,200, compared to €330,400 for two-adult households where at least one adult is aged 65 or over'. So, if we start there, investments would be key. A lot of people of an older generation don't necessarily know how to invest as a retiree, as distinct to somebody who is working. People might say, 'Well, I have X amount, and I'm only ever going to have X amount, so therefore this is the only pool that I've got.' Yes, but if someone is 65, the likelihood of them living to 75 or even 85 is quite high, so you can still potentially have an investment horizon of as much as 20 years. An easy rule of thumb is that you should have your age in bonds in a portfolio, so the older you get, the less risk you take. If I was to follow this rule of thumb and I was 70, I'd have 70 per cent in bonds and then might invest the remaining 30 per cent in the stock market. The global stock market has generated around 10 per cent return annually since 1926, but of course this is an average.

Q: That makes sense, but what if you have a bad year and lose money that you can't afford to lose at an older age?
A: Well, if you have money that you can't afford to potentially lose, don't put it at risk. However, if you can afford a bad year, you can apply a 'euro cost averaging' approach. What this means is that you buy into good-quality companies regularly over a period of time. If you buy a fund, then its strategy should re-adapt to take on the opportunities of a better year. However, watch out for fund costs and ensure that you talk to a reputable financial advisor.

Q: Can that mean investing some of your pension lump sum? A lot of people get confused about how much and what to do with it.

A: There is always a different approach to investing a lump sum and being a regular investor. A regular investor will get some highs and some lows, but the aforementioned euro cost averaging can even things out. A lump sum investor needs to be more aware of timing the market. This is particularly important when investing a pension lump sum. Do your research if this is your plan and seek further financial advice.

Q: Now, back to that second point. What else can we do as older people to manage our money – say, to help the younger generation?

A: Well, the second area relates to tax and specifically to inheritance tax. A lot of people don't realise that there's a small-gift exemption available in Ireland, where you can give up to €3,000 tax free to anyone. Now, if you bought a house in the 1980s, say, for €30,000 and it's now worth €800,000 and you're going to leave it to your son or daughter who already has their own home, they will breach the threshold for paying inheritance tax, which is €335,000 at the time of writing – they will need to pay tax on anything above that ... What I'm saying here is, plan your inheritance – realise what your assets are actually worth and understand that there are actually ways to minimise your tax liability legally and ethically.

Q: That's good news! And the third way in which you can manage your money?
A: The third one applies to anyone at any age. It looks at ways in which you can save money really easily. At the moment, I'm reviewing my gas and electricity suppliers, like everyone else in the country, but what about your direct debits? You can look them up with a few taps of a button online, and you might find yourself saying, 'I can't believe that I have a direct debit for that!' I like to say that it's about putting managing your money on autopilot. You can have a specific time every month or every year to check on your spending and on what your entitlements are to benefits, particularly when you get to over 70. For example, I contacted my health insurance provider recently and asked if there were any penalties for paying by monthly direct debit, and they said no. So, I figure, why pay €3,500 for two of us when I can pay it more easily monthly? It's about managing cash flow.

The point about tech is that it can help you to manage your money easily, but it's also there to be enjoyed. It can help you feel more connected to people you love, help you find out information quicker and find new sources of enjoyment. My parents didn't want to know anything about technology until my brother and I got them an iPad and smartphone for Christmas. Now, Mam watches the analysis of her favourite soccer team online and looks at YouTube videos of places we've been on holidays. Dad sends in condolences on RIP.ie and reads *The Examiner* on the internet. They're delighted with themselves! Give it a chance and you might be surprised at what you find!

Q: That's an excellent point, Susan. Any other tips?

A: I think the most important would be to set up what we call Enduring Power of Attorney (EPA) early. Safeguarding Ireland (www.safeguardingireland.org) has published a report on the prevalence of financial abuse of older people, and, unfortunately, it is an issue in hundreds of homes across the country, because the elderly are vulnerable. So, setting up Enduring Power of Attorney needs to be done early, holistically and with certain safeguards in place. For example, controlling who has viewing access, because I find that older people can be extremely trusting and can assume that other people know how to do these things. So, Power of Attorney is an awful lot more than thinking about what happens if something happens: it's about understanding what exactly it implies. The courts website – https://

www.courts.ie/general-information-enduring-powers-attorney – has a very simple explanation of what EPA means, but my take on it is, who do you want to step in to make decisions and take actions for you, if you mentally can't? I'm guessing you have somebody that springs straight to mind and a person whom you trust.

Q: Of course, that's good to know. But how can I make sure that my nearest and dearest are looked after in the event of my dying?
A: Well, it's not just about having a will: it's about reviewing it. You might say, well, the will was made five years ago, but the value of the house might have changed, there might be new grandchildren, circumstances might have changed, as might the mental clarity or the ability of someone to make those decisions. Sometimes, we might look at something we did a while ago and think, I can't believe how much has changed. The time to have that conversation is not at a time when we're in an anxious environment, whether it's a funeral or whether it is in deep grief or whether it is potentially one of shock. They're not times to be arguing over things. Instead, these types of conversations can be positive, you know – they can be very considerate and very thoughtful. The opposite is to die 'intestate', that is, without a will, and it's very difficult for the next of

kin who have to make decisions for you and they can't talk to you.

Q: That sounds like very sensible advice. But one issue that a lot of people ask me about is that of 'leaving it too late' to start a pension. Is it ever too late?

A: I would say, no, it's not too late. If I was, say, 40, and I had a pension for one month and put €100 into it, and I'm classed as a 'high earner' and that's actually your average person on the average wage of €44,202, you are going to get the tax back from the government. In other words, the incentive that the government has for you or I to save for our old age is they give us the tax back that we would pay in a normal payslip. So, you're a 40-year-old and you have 25 or 26 years of those pension contributions to get the opportunity cost of their tax back and get the benefits of the aggregated investment returns and they can grow tax free. So, no, you haven't left it too late if you're a 40-year-old, or a 50-year-old or even a 60-year-old!

Q: Really?

A: Yes! You'll get the tax relief from the government on the way in and you'll get the investment returns. Now, if you're a 60-year-old, you might not want to take much risk in terms of investment, but those investments are free of tax, so there's a net positive benefit. However, you can't magic up an income after saving for 2 years out of 30. There will be a pool of money there that will be worth something, but you won't be sailing around the Caribbean. But when I look at pension systems around the world, Ireland has a very generous system in terms of contributions from the government. But I like the Australian system of auto-enrolment from your first pay cheque, which means that you have to opt out if you don't wish to pay. And an awful lot of issues to do with pensions are to do with inertia – 'Ah, sure, I'll look at it next month.' I see that Zurich has reported on the auto-enrolment system as follows: 'scheduled to go live from the first quarter of 2024 [it] will mean that all employees not already contributing to an existing employer pension scheme who are aged between 23 and 60 and earning €20,000 or more across all employments, will be required to automatically enrol in the new scheme'.

Q: And am I right in thinking that the pension situation is worse for women?
A: Yes. The last time I looked, the ESRI estimated that the pension pay gap was 35 per cent, so for every euro a man was getting from his pension, a woman would be getting 35 cent less. Part of that is due to gaps, and to the choices that a woman might make to look after children or elderly relatives, but the self-employed woman is the least likely of the working population to

have a pension, and that can be due to the inactivity of women in this area – and perhaps to being more used to making short-term financial decisions, such as the household budget, and traditionally the man has been seen to make the longer-term ones. It's about changing that mindset.

Q: But what happens if I just don't have the money? For many of us, there's precious little left at the end of the month.

A: Of course, but what exactly do we mean when we say 'no money'? For example, if I set up a PRSA, which is a Personal Retirement Savings Account, I need €300 per year to pay into that account – not €10,000.

– Staying Safe Online –

Now that you've digested Susan's excellent advice, we'll take a deep breath and look at the issue of online safety for older people. We all grew up in the era of the bank manager and the cheque book, so for many of us online banking and shopping can be quite daunting. But it can also be a really fast and efficient way to bank and a convenient way to order groceries and clothing. No more calling into the branch manager to apply for a loan or going to the bank to lodge a cheque! No more wrestling with outfits in a busy changing room! The trouble can arise when we are trying to pay bills simply, when we have a problem and need to chat to someone, God help us, or when we see an unfamiliar text or email from the bank that's requesting account details or suggesting that we click on a link. How can we enjoy the benefits of our new fast-paced system and stay safe?

For a start, take matters into your own hands when it comes to online safety and to your own computer and online literacy. Look up organisations that help the elderly and study the information they have about online safety. Talk to your bank – pay them a visit! – and ask them to talk you through their safety protocols. Many banks have online tutorials on internet safety and lots of people use them, not just us oldies! For example, Age UK – www.ageuk.org.uk – has some excellent advice on online banking and shopping safety. They look at the importance of creating a strong password (you can do this using Google Password Manager, for example, which will generate and remember passwords for you), using a good virus protector on your laptop or tablet, and password-protecting your mobile phone and your wireless router – that's the box in the corner that controls your Wi-Fi. It should have a password on it already so that others can't access your home Wi-Fi, but, if you're not sure, double-check with your internet provider.

Mobile phones have changed our lives, but they come with lots of fun and games for older people like myself! Passwords are really being replaced now by other, more secure methods of protecting your mobile, but some people have told me that they find the fingerprint-recognition on their mobiles difficult, because their fingers might wobble or shake. Try facial recognition instead, so the phone can only be opened when you hold it up to your face. Alternatively, get a phone that is simpler to use for older people. You don't have to have a 'stupid phone', as a friend of mine calls it! You can get a smartphone with larger icons, louder sound and easier-to-manage features. Or you can get a smartphone but use only the apps that you'll need – think about what you want from a smartphone before buying one and go in to the mobile phone provider and ask them for advice. Many providers have information on buying phones that suit older people – for example, Three's *The Ultimate Guide to Buying a Phone for Older People*.

When it comes to purchasing online, it suits many of us to do so, because we might find it hard to get out to the shops. It's so easy and convenient once you get the hang of it. However, many of us worry about fraud. The good news is that the vast majority of high-street names have easy-to-use websites and good security in place. The things to look out for are pop-up windows that might appear on-screen and direct you to another (less reputable) site, or links that invite you to click on them. My rule of thumb is don't click on any links online. Instead, go directly to that retailer's website so you'll know that it's legitimate. And if you get an email purporting to be from your bank, look at it carefully. If it's not legitimate, it'll have misspellings or ask for your account details. Your bank will never ask for these, so the chances are it's not real. If in doubt, don't reply: either bin it or leave it untouched and ask a savvy younger relation to take a look. Keep your passwords safe, and don't use the same password on a number of sites. Use a password generator (you can also use Google Password Manager for this) to come up with something really fiendish!

Another good tip that came from Age UK was to use one card for your online purchases, which makes it simpler to see if there is anything suspicious. A credit or debit card will offer you an additional level of protection via the 'chargeback' process. This means that if you don't receive the coat or handbag you ordered, you can request a refund from the retailer and, if they won't or can't oblige, from the card issuer. Moneyguide Ireland has a very helpful explanation of the process here: https://www.moneyguideireland.com/protection-when-buying-with-debit-or-credit-cards.html. A friend of mine uses PayPal, which is a very simple payment system, but which offers added protection. It's linked to your current account and is easy to set up.

Having read all of the above, you might well think that the online world is a minefield and people are only waiting to get hold of our details, but remember, as Susan suggested in our chat, it can also be a window onto the world for those of us who might be less mobile. We can keep in touch with people on the other side of the world via Zoom, we can shop until we drop and we can bank efficiently and with so much more ease than we could before. Don't let your worries prevent you from surfing happily. All you have to do is be mindful. And for goodness sake don't be embarrassed if you've been caught out. It happens to us all nowadays. The important thing is to keep up to date and to ask for help from trusted people in your world – from your bank, for example. You're a valued customer, and they'll be happy to offer advice.

In Ireland, there are a number of organisations that offer training in computer skills for older people: Age Action offers *Getting Started: Computer Training*; Active Retirement and Alone Ireland are offering *Hi Digital*, a programme sponsored by Vodafone that helps older people to learn computer skills (www.hidigital.ie/en); and Generation Tech helps elderly people with computer issues (www.generationtech.ie). They have a helpline that operates Monday to Friday, 8 a.m. to 8 p.m., and you can email them at INeedHelp@generationtech.ie. You can even 'DM' them – that's Direct Message to you – on Twitter! What better way to be tech savvy!

8.

Going Home

'In this world, nothing can be said
to be certain, except death and taxes.'

Benjamin Franklin

If you're like me, you'll have given the subject of death a bit of thought, not just in practical terms, but also emotionally. You can't shy away from it, because it simply is part of our reality at this age. Whether you are losing friends or relatives, or inching towards the departure lounge yourself, death is indeed part of life once we get older.

The business of dying has changed a lot over the last half-century. When I was a child, it was often said that someone had 'dropped dead' suddenly – usually of a heart attack or some other sudden event. People smoked more and succumbed to diseases like emphysema, like my poor dad. Nowadays, with improvements in medicine, older people are more likely to die after a period of illness or decline, perhaps going in and out of hospital for treatment. This really focuses the mind.

In addition, many of us won't be as connected to death and the dying as we once were, when people died and were waked at home. Also, until quite recently, many people's religious belief was that, when people died, they were going to their 'eternal reward' in Heaven. So death was not 'the end', as such, but simply a staging post. In some religions, people die and return as someone or something else. Many of us believe in the spirit world and in angels and so on, and some of us have even had near-death experiences in which we feel that we've gained some understanding of what it is to die. But even more of us believe that death is the end and that we'll simply return to the earth.

– Death Rituals Around the World –

In Tibet, the bodies of the dead are left outside to be eaten by animals, and, while this might sound cruel to us, they do this so that the soul of the person is allowed to fly to

Heaven more easily and the cycle of life is complete. In South Korea, people's ashes are transformed into colourful beads with which you decorate your home. And if you think that the Irish have all the answers when it comes to death rituals, the Filipinos are way ahead of us, with many and varied traditions, including dressing the dead person in their finest clothes and sitting them up in an armchair with a cigarette in their mouth, hanging coffins from cliffs so that they are closer to God and dressing children in red to ward off evil spirits. In Ghana, people's coffins are often personalised to say something about their lives, with sometimes spectacular results. There are coffins in the shape of aeroplanes or giant shoes, lions or eagles, and it has become increasingly popular to hire a dance troupe to carry the coffin. Some of the dancing can seem quite jaunty, but, as funerals are very important social occasions, families want to do their very best for their loved ones. Of course, probably the most famous festival of the dead is the Mexican Día de los Muertos, or Day of the Dead. In this mix of Aztec and Spanish rituals, the dead return to Earth for one day, during which they are feted with offerings of sweets and marigold flowers, and altars are made at home in their honour. People also gather at cemeteries to tend to the graves and commune with their dead loved ones, and of course the streets are festooned with elaborate papier mâché skeletons to remind people that death is never far away.

Before the Catholic Church became involved in the funeral rite, there were many different kinds of funerals in Ireland, too. Many of us will have been to Newgrange or to other passage tombs in Ireland, and we know that they were burial chambers for the people of Neolithic times. However, what the burial rites involved, we're not entirely sure. I came across a study of the Carrowkeel passage tombs in County Sligo, conducted by the University of Otago in New Zealand. According to Dr Johnny Geber, the ritual might have included 'the bodies of the dead being "processed" by their kin and community in various ways, including cremation and dismemberment. It was probably done with the goal to help the souls of the dead to reach the next stages of their existence'. So what might seem grisly to us was simply to hasten the passage of the dead to the afterlife.

Frank McNally wrote about another Irish custom in 'An Irish Diary' in the *Irish Times* in 2022, that of '*trí coiscéim na marbh*' or 'three steps with the dead', in which people would accompany the dead, even just for a little while, to their resting place. Interestingly, the custom seems to be a Dublin one. However, there were any number of superstitions associated with death and the dying in Ireland. According to https://www.askaboutireland.ie/

reading-room/history-heritage/folklore-of-ireland/
folklore-in-ireland/the-life-cycle/death/, 'It was
often considered bad luck to visit somebody when
returning from a funeral, most likely because it was
considered that the dead, or the fairies, were more
likely to be present at that time and thus "take" the
sick person. Every effort was made to keep the fire
stoked, with its glowing embers symbolising the life
of the patient. As death nears, efforts were made to
ease their passage. The doors and windows were
opened. Sometimes, a hole was made in the wall
or thatched roof to allow the spirit to escape. The
person was sometimes taken from the bed and laid
on straw on the floor, the idea being that the wild
bird's feather could prolong the struggle.' And if you
were lucky enough to die at Christmas time, 'the
gates of Heaven stayed open during this time and
sinners could enter freely'.

Lady Jane Francesca Wilde – or 'Speranza', to use
her pen name – wrote a book called *Ancient Legends,
Mystic Charms and Superstitions of Ireland* in 1888,
which is now in the National Library. In this book,
she collected a range of stories of folk beliefs in this
country. One section was about death and the stories
associated with it. Commonly, people believed that the
dead had been carried away by the fairies and that any
contact with fairies would hasten your own passing.
The stories are quite haunting, if you'll excuse the

pun: in one, a fisherman is out on the sea one day when he comes across a boat with three other men in it. One look at them tells him that they are dead, because he recognises them as the ghosts of three friends who drowned the year before. He follows instructions to cast his line, and he catches a huge fish and takes it home, taking care not to look at his three friends again for fear he would be taken with them. When he gets home, the locals tell him that if only he'd looked, he could have saved the three souls and restored them to their families.

I was captivated by a description of 'the Irish ullaloo' in a piece I came across on my travels; this was a kind of lament. When your loved one died, you would hire a bard to lead the funeral attendees in a lament for the deceased, and when a funeral procession would pass a house in the country, the ladies would emit a kind of howl. That must have been very cathartic! In *Castle Rackrent*, the writer Maria Edgeworth recalled that, 'This gives notice to the inhabitants of the village that a funeral is passing, and immediately they flock out to follow it. In the province of Munster it is a common thing for the women to follow a funeral, to join the universal cry with all their might and main for some time, and then to turn and ask, "Arrah! Who is it that's dead? Who is it we're crying for?"'

Many of these traditions faded when the Catholic Church became involved in funerals around the time of the Famine, and they began to take on the shape that we are familiar with today. However, one ancient Irish tradition that still persists is that of the wake. In this ritual, the dead person is dressed in their finest clothing and laid out in the good room for family and locals to pay their respects. It's less common in cities nowadays, but still very much practised in the countryside. I have attended many wakes, and I like the sense in which the dead and the living are in the same space, as if dying is just a slightly different state. People stand around and chat and admire the deceased, and say that they haven't looked as well in ages, and generally have time to come to terms with the deceased's passing and to remember happy times they spent with them.

– Preparing for Death –

We're probably a lot more separate from death than we used to be, now that it's no longer an everyday part of our lives. In the late nineteenth and early twentieth centuries, people expected to lose a child to illness and to die themselves at a relatively young age. If disease or poverty didn't kill them, they were very fortunate indeed. Now, because so many of us live to a ripe old age, we almost don't expect that death will be at the end of it. Many of us even fear death. There's a word for that fear – *thanatophobia*. Interestingly, we can fear death more if we have no religious belief, according to some studies, and I suppose this makes sense when death is more of a full stop than a semicolon, if you see what I mean. But while thanatophobia refers to an extreme fear of dying, many of us are afraid, not so much of death itself, but of the way in which we might die. I came across an article recently which looked at our fear of death and how this compared with the feelings of those who were actually facing it. It was called 'Dying Is Unexpectedly Positive'. It was a very detailed study with lots of maths involved, but the digested read, which was in *The Guardian* newspaper, explained that it involved two groups of people, one of which was writing online about their experiences of dying from cancer or ALS (motor neurone disease) while the other group was told to imagine they had a terminal illness and to write about it. The results showed that those who were actually facing death experienced less fear around it. As one academic, Havi Carel of the University of Bristol, commented: 'I think you get used to the idea of dying, like we get accustomed to many things. The initial shock after receiving a poor prognosis is horrific, but after months or years of living with this knowledge, the dread subsides.'

Do you think that's true? Like so many people, I suppose I haven't given the idea of my death a lot of thought, apart from hoping that it is a peaceful one. Many of us would prefer to die peacefully at home, and not in hospital or in a nursing home. A study in the Netherlands concluded that while a majority of elderly interviewees expressed a preference to die at home, that actually changed over time and with the progression of their illness. Many people ultimately preferred to have any pain or discomfort eased, rather than to die at home.

– The Practical Things –

I was talking to a friend of mine recently, and she recalled her grandmother making elaborate arrangements in the event of her sudden death. The woman was 80 and about to go on a trip to the United States, but insisted that my friend and her mum call over first so she could show them where all her paperwork was. She was convinced that she wouldn't return from her trip. She lived to be 92 ...

Maybe we don't really want to think about this, but planning for our death will really help our loved ones. There'll be no guesswork or financial distress, and everyone will know exactly what you wanted. You can start by making sure that you've made a will and, if you have, that it's up to date. You can also nominate a person to make medical decisions on your behalf, should you be too unwell to do so. This is called an Advanced Healthcare Directive (AHD). In it, you can detail your wishes about any future treatment and whether, for example, you wish to prolong your life in certain circumstances. Not wishing to have your life prolonged is not the same as assisted dying, by the way, in which medication is taken specifically to cause death and which isn't legal in Ireland, although it is in some other countries, such as Belgium and Switzerland. The AHD is a legal document and it may sound alarming, but imagine if you were unable to make those decisions yourself? I'm sure you would like to spare your relatives any confusion or upset by making clear what you would like to happen.

The Irish Hospice Foundation has a very useful and thorough planning tool called the Think Ahead Plan and the pack is available here: www.hospicefoundation.ie/i-need-help/i-want-to-think-ahead/get-my-think-ahead-planning-pack/. It includes three booklets: one sets out your wishes for future care; the second is your Advance Healthcare Directive, onto which you can record your wishes and have them witnessed by two people, thus making it legally binding; and the third sets out your medical requirements in summary, which you can give to your GP. It'll then be stored in your records.

According to the Hospice Foundation, three-quarters of us would like to die at home, but only a quarter of us actually do so. This can be for any number of reasons, but they stress that 'a good death' can happen in a variety of settings, from hospitals, some now equipped with better facilities for end-of-life care, to nursing homes and the Caru programme, which enables nursing-home staff to learn more about how to help the dying and their families, to home itself, when a specially trained nurse can help the person dying to manage discomfort and offer support to relatives.

If your will is up to date, and you have organised your Enduring Power of Attorney, make sure that you have a full list of your bank accounts and any other policies, such as life insurance, at hand so that it can be found easily.

Many of us who wish to be buried in a grave will already have purchased a plot, because they are at a premium nowadays. However, if you are going to be cremated, you might like to tell your loved ones where you would like your ashes scattered. Perhaps you would like them interred in a 'columbarium', which is a mini-graveyard, if you like, where your ashes can be stored with your name and dates in a plaque on the front. Some people want to have them scattered in a place that was special to them; others would prefer to remain at home in an urn. Whatever you'd like to do, have a think about it and let others know. The Hospice Foundation even mentions burial at sea, and the Department of Transport has a list of requirements for that, believe it or not – but for many reasons, cremation followed by scattering of ashes at sea is preferred.

– Saying Goodbye –

Have you thought about what kind of funeral you'd like to have? I always think that is an odd question, because I'll be unaware of the proceedings! But if you think about it, funerals are really for the bereaved, not the deceased. Many of us have some idea of music or prayers or whether we'd like a religious or secular funeral. With religious funerals, the formatting is already there, of course, but you might have wishes for a particular song or prayer, or for certain gifts to be brought up to the altar. I always think that there's a comfort to religious services, a sense of a familiar rite that has been performed over and over again for centuries.

If you'll be having a secular funeral or humanist service, a specially trained minister will conduct the service, inviting people to speak, to reminisce, to play a particular song or tell a story about you. I have been to a number of these services and they are lovely, full of warmth and positive memories. A friend of mine told me about one that she'd been to for a local man in her neighbourhood who had led a short and somewhat sad life, and she always remembers what the minister said at his service. 'Sometimes, it's enough just to have lived.' Isn't that wonderful? It reminded her that everyone's life is special, even if it is only to one or two people, and everyone is loved by somebody.

Another friend of mine will be arranging a memorial service for her parents, because they have both opted to donate their bodies to science, just like my own father did. I also remember a story my sister Kate told me about a man who came in to the Royal College of Surgeons, where she worked for many years. He was very elderly and really not up to the journey from west Dublin, but he was determined to donate his body to science, so he'd come in to ask what he needed to do. Kate talked him through the process and he actually came back again to sign forms, in spite of his old age and frailty. When she heard some time later that he'd died in his garden and had needed an autopsy, she was devastated for him, because if you need one, you can't donate your body to science.

If this is something you have chosen, then you'll know that each institution has helpful guidance for relatives as to what will happen to their loved ones. For example, in Trinity College, a family room is provided for relatives and friends to say goodbye to their loved one, and their remains are returned after three years so that relatives can inter them. There is also a Book of Remembrance for all those who donate their bodies to medical science, which is a wonderful thing to do. If you would like to donate your body to science, you can contact the relevant department in one of the five institutions that study bodies for medical purposes: Trinity College Dublin, University College Dublin, the Royal College of Surgeons, University College Cork and NUIG. This link will connect you directly to the institutions' donor pages: https://hospicefoundation.ie/i-need-help/i-want-to-think-ahead/care-after-death/considering-organ-or-body-donation/

– The Occasion Itself –

Even if the person has led a long and happy life, their funeral can be a stressful, emotional time for their loved ones. When I was reading up on funeral traditions, I came across a piece by a Ghanaian journalist, Elizabeth Ohene, in which she spoke of her frustration that funerals there took so long. It has to do with the extended family, it would seem, who take over the funeral arrangements from close relatives – and you can imagine what it must be like having to please a huge crowd of people. The wrangling can go on for some months and, in fact, if you short-circuit this process it's considered to be sacrilege. It's good to know that feeling the stress isn't confined to Ireland!

Whatever issues you might have with family, I would try to put them to one side, just for the duration of the funeral and the gathering afterwards. If you haven't spoken to your cousin John in 10 years, don't pick now to get things off your chest. Try to focus on the fact that this is a celebration of your loved one's life and you know that they'd hate for there to be any conflict. Try to come together as a family, even if it's only for a day or two. Listen to each other's point of view as respectfully as you can and make decisions accordingly. Of course, not everyone will be happy, but try to accommodate as many opinions and wishes as possible. Share the tasks out as democratically as you can, giving everyone a part in the service, and try to ignore any comments that aren't relevant to the funeral itself, such as asking about wills or estates. You can simply say, 'We'll get to that after the funeral.' Try to keep your focus on 'now' and not on things that might have happened many years ago. I know that this might be hard!

At the funeral itself, you may be given the opportunity to remember your loved one in a eulogy. Before you deliver it, have a think about what your relative would have liked you to say about them. If they struggled with something, it's fine to allude to that, while not needing to pore over the details, but don't ignore it either, in case it becomes the elephant in the room. Focus on their strengths and the things they loved, whether it was a fondness for jokes or a love of *Mastermind* or hiking. Everyone has something that marks them out as special.

Your funeral director will help you with all of the big decisions that come with planning a funeral, from the removal to the reposing to the service itself, along with the choice of burial. They can help with selecting hymns and readings, arranging flowers, a book of condolence and so on. Bear in mind that a funeral can cost anywhere between €3,000 and €8,000. This often comes as a shock to people, but many of us put money aside to pay for a funeral and this makes sense. There are some funeral plans, or life insurance plans that will help you save for a funeral, but if the family really can't afford one, they can apply for an Additional Needs Payment from their local social welfare office. If the death is as a result of an accident connected with work, a funeral grant can be applied for. You might also like to know that a Widowed or Surviving Civil Partner Grant is available to those who qualify. This is a one-off payment to help with funeral costs and other expenses around a death. You can find out more by contacting your local Intreo office or Citizens Information.

Whatever the situation for the person who is dying, they will ultimately be at peace. But their friends, relatives, spouse or partner will have to carry on without them. This became painfully clear to many of us during Covid when so many people died without their loved ones present. Sometimes, we might wonder how we'll cope without our other half or parent, or indeed anyone close to us, and bereavement is very much a process, as I discovered myself when Mum died.

Psychiatrist Elizabeth Kübler-Ross developed a theory that we go through a number of stages in the grieving process: 1. Shock, 2. Denial, 3. Anger, 4. Bargaining, 5. Depression, 6. Acceptance and 7. Processing. Do you recognise any of them in your own journey? I can certainly relate to feelings of shock. I knew Mum was going to die at some point – she was 97 after all – but even so, the shock of her passing really hit me. I wasn't ready for it at all. I don't think any of us are, no matter how much time we have to prepare.

By 'denial', this doesn't mean that you don't accept that your loved one has gone – it's simply that it doesn't seem real. You think that they will walk in the door at any moment, and accepting that they've gone and are never returning seems impossible.

'Anger' is something many of us will relate to, that feeling of rage that we've been left alone to get on with life without our loved one. It's perfectly normal, even if some of us find it very uncomfortable. Sometimes, we might even feel angry with ourselves: that we're not 'getting on with things' or getting over our loss. But there's no timetable here, and there's no 'right' time to move on.

'Bargaining' means wishing and hoping for another chance to make things right. Maybe you had a row with your loved one before they left the house and you think, *If only I could talk to them just once and apologise*; or perhaps you feel that you didn't do enough for them while they were alive. Again, these feelings of guilt are entirely normal.

Sometimes, if we're feeling very upset and full of emotion, we can end up feeling quite down and alone with our grief. It's as if the world doesn't quite understand us. At this stage, don't be afraid to reach out and seek help. Talk to someone about what you're feeling, and don't think that you have to bear it alone. Many people will have travelled the same road that you're travelling and will be happy to listen. And, of course, there are professional grief counsellors there to help – visiting one is not a sign of failure: quite the opposite. You are taking control of your own grief and asking someone else to guide you as you process it and progress to the stage at which you accept your loved one's departure. At this point, you might start reaching out to friends and family again and reconnecting with the world. This is perfectly normal: as humans, we are designed to be part of the living world, but don't be afraid if you 'slip back' into one stage or another as you grieve – grief really isn't a linear process, and the above are simple guideposts, not a prescription.

If you would like to share how you're feeling, you can reach out to the Irish Hospice Foundation, which has a helpline: 1800 80 70 77; another organisation that helps those who have lost loved ones to suicide is Pieta at 1800 247 247 and the Samaritans at 116 123. If your query isn't urgent, but you would like support, they also have an app with all kinds of helpful content at selfhelp. samaritans.org. www.widow.ie is an online support service which helps widowers and partners, too.

It's a serious subject, of course, but I thought I'd end with something a little more light-hearted. I'm not sure if you remember *The School Around the Corner*? It was a TV show hosted by teacher Paddy Crosbie – and later by Gerry Ryan. Apparently, it was the most popular show in Ireland in the early 1960s. A few years ago, they found some archive footage of one of the early shows in Cork, where a little boy stood up to sing a song, belting out the words to 'Come Down from the Mountain, Katy Deary' and was rewarded with a toy gun. I don't think that would happen nowadays!

Anyway, I remember one story that Crosbie told about teaching in inner-city Dublin. One of the pupils, let's call him Johnny, wasn't particularly academic, shall we say, and Crosbie often wondered what would become of him. Years later, Crosbie was walking along the street when he came across the same Johnny, looking very smart.

'Johnny,' he exclaimed. 'Don't you look great – what are you at now?'

'Oh, I work for a local undertaker,' Johnny said proudly.

'And what exactly do you do?' Crosbie enquired.

'Oh, I go along before the remains are viewed and I tidy things up a bit. In fact, I'm heading to Benburb Street now, because a gentleman has just died up there, if you want to come along.'

Paddy thought, *Maybe I should go, because it might be interesting to see what Johnny is up to now.* So off they both went and arrived a little while later at a terraced house, with a little front door and two windows, one up and one down. Johnny knocked at the door, and when it was opened there was a lot of whispering as he announced that he was from the undertaker, and the two of them stepped into the hall. The woman of the house ushered them up the stairs and, curious, Paddy followed Johnny up to the landing. There were three closed doors. Johnny opened the first one, and the room was empty. 'Not that one then,' said Johnny.

He opened the next one and, lo and behold, there was the corpse in the bed.

They both went into the room and looked around, and Paddy Crosbie noticed that the deceased was lying in bed with his knees up. 'What are you going to do now, Johnny?'

'What do you mean?' Johnny replied.

'Well, you know, rigor mortis and all that,' said Paddy.

'Oh, that's not a problem,' Johnny said proudly. 'Just stand back.'

Paddy stood back and Johnny picked up a chair that'd been pushed against the wall. He lifted it high above his head and brought it down with an almighty crash on the two knees to straighten them. Whereupon the corpse leaped up in the bed with an almighty howl. He wasn't dead at all – he was just having 40 winks – and the deceased was in the bedroom next door! Poor Johnny. All of Paddy's worst fears for him were confirmed ...

9.

Francis's Twenty Tips for Growing Old Gracefully – and with Joy!

1. Remember to have fun. I'd put this top of my list. As we get older, we can forget, with all our responsibilities and obligations, to enjoy ourselves. The other thing is that we're inclined to think in terms of 'musts' – I must post that letter/do my tax return/email Mary. The next time you hear yourself using that expression, stop and think, *What do I want to do?* You can still write the letter and so on, but put fun first, for once. A friend of mine loves to dance around the kitchen to Marvin Gaye and Tammi Terrell, and why not? Sure, who's looking? Her husband's used to it anyway! Another friend of mine loves watching *Who Wants*

to Be a Millionaire with a cup of tea and a chocolate biscuit, answering all the questions and asking herself what she'd do if she won the million. I love dressing up and going out to dinner. I don't drink, but I still love the food and the atmosphere. That's my idea of fun. Yours might be lawn bowls or a round of golf, but I won't hold that against you! Make it a daily thing, even if it's just for half an hour. It'll make you feel so much better.

2. There's been a lot of talk about 'self-care' recently, and sometimes it makes me groan, but the point of it is a good one. If we don't take care of ourselves, we won't be fit and healthy to enjoy life to its fullest. We'll feel less than our best if we don't eat nourishing, tasty food and, Lord knows, we don't need to spend any more time at the doctor's. There's nothing we can do if we've inherited Dad's gammy knee, but as Dr Mark Rowe said, we can control the other 80 per cent of our health, and that's a lot. Take care of yourself.

3. Try to get quality sleep. I'm a night owl, and I think nothing of texting or watching a movie or reading until 1 a.m. It suits me, but I fully recognise the fact that I probably don't get enough sleep. So, while I still get up relatively early, I'm trying to go to bed just a half an hour earlier and to leave the devices in the living room. I won't be buying one of those smart watches, though. A friend of

mine has one and it's always telling him how much REM sleep he's had, which would make me even more anxious.

4. I was highly amused to read an article recently that asked, 'When do I know if I'm too old to do something?' My watchword is, you're never too old, provided you work with your body and understand its limitations. The article recommended not taking up skateboarding or climbing because of the risk of falls, but I'm not in favour of absolutes myself. If you've always enjoyed climbing, for example, you can still do it, but it might take a little longer because your feet aren't as flexible, and you might also need to think before you make a risky move, because your recovery time will be longer. It's about balancing caution with the high that comes from trying new things. If you've always wanted to try paragliding, go with an instructor; if you want to surf, learn how to surf, but understand that you might not be leaping up on the board like the youngsters.

5. Some of us love a party and there's no reason on earth why we shouldn't continue, but being the last person to leave ...? Well, maybe leave that to the youngsters! Our bodies aren't as good at metabolising alcohol when we get older, so our tolerance will be less, and we'll certainly feel it the morning after, and sometimes the morning after that!

6. If you act old, you'll feel old. My friend Frank will kill me for saying this, but every time he gets out of a chair, he moans and groans like an old man. According to *The Sun*, the three main signifiers of ageing are the moaning and groaning when getting out of a chair, forgetting things and looking for your glasses when they're on top of your head. That's why I wear mine on a chain around my neck … Mind you, other signifiers were 'wearing socks and sandals at the same time' and 'developing a taste for sherry'. I'm not sure how scientific the poll was!

7. Try not to get set in your ways. I used to enjoy a TV show called *Grumpy Old Men*. It was basically grumpy old men – and women – giving out about the things they didn't like about modern life, and it made me laugh. But getting set in your ways is less funny, because it really takes the joy out of life. If you find yourself saying 'In my day …' or 'Young people nowadays are so rude …' or developing a fixed perspective on how the world should work, maybe it's time that you shook up your ideas. Have you ever wondered why you have a particular habit or way of behaving and asked yourself if it still fits you? Try changing things up a little bit.

8. Use words that are neither too 'down with the kids' nor old-fashioned. It can be a tricky balance, but 'my bad' and 'I'm very excited for the new

Star Wars movie' are probably best left to those under 21! I loved a few examples that I came across online. Would young people ever send a 'Dear John' letter to each other if they wanted to get out of a relationship? I don't think so. And as for 'Goodnight, John Boy' and referring to someone as a 'wet blanket' – no ... Obsolete, I'm afraid, but at least you'll give young people a laugh trying to explain them.

9. Call (I'm showing my age), text or drop a line to a friend every day. The older I get, the more thankful I am for my friends. There's nothing more relaxing than chatting to someone who has known you forever, nor more stimulating than getting to know someone new.

10. Try to get on with your other half and be patient. My married friends have asked me for this one! Yes, you'll have heard all the stories before; you will be familiar with all of the aforementioned moaning and groaning/loss of hearing/driving very slowly and so on, but try to appreciate what you have. Growing old together is a great blessing in a world that's full of loneliness.

11. Connect with younger people. That way, you'll see that they don't have horns! Apart from that, they will challenge your thinking and introduce you to new things. Thanks to my nieces and nephews, I'm now familiar with various 'memes' and I know

how to 'binge watch' Netflix. But I also like to think that young people can get something out of the interaction, too. Maybe you can help them with their worries or concerns because you'll have been there before?

12. Do small things outside your comfort zone. Eleanor Roosevelt used to say, 'Try one thing that scares you every day.' Every day might be a little daunting, but the principle is a good one. I think when we get older that we can settle into a nice, comfortable pattern in life and almost be afraid to try new things. Even if it's simply taking a new route to work or trying a new hobby, give it a go to get those neurons firing.

13. Be comfortable in your own skin. Do you remember when we were younger, how self-conscious we were? We were always worrying what people thought about us. Now, we couldn't care less – or, at least, I couldn't. That's a great gift that comes with growing older.

14. Take a few risks. At a certain stage in life, we can feel that our best days are behind us. Maybe we would like to have set up a café but the timing wasn't right, or we wanted to be a teacher but didn't have the qualifications. Why not try it now? Nowadays, we can all have second acts. But make your risk-taking sensible. Maybe don't plough your life savings into a café on a whim. Instead,

take a holiday and work in a café to get the experience, or offer to do shifts in a little food truck at the weekends to get a feel for how it all works. Fill in for the owner while they're on holiday, and so on.

And if you want to be a teacher, see if it's doable and, if so, how. You might not need a degree plus a master's in education to teach in a particular area if you have specialist skills, or you could look into teaching English as a volunteer.

15. Save up for a rainy day. As life will have taught all of us, anything can happen, so have a little account somewhere that will keep you going for a while if needed.

16. Get those photos of your nieces and nephews, children and grandchildren, framed and put them on the wall to remind you of everything you have. If you're like me, you'll have tons of snaps on your phone, but if you really want to enjoy them, send them off to a printing service and get them framed.

17. Accept that you're older. Some of us find this difficult because our society is so youth oriented, and maybe because we're a bit afraid of it, but old age can be freeing. You no longer have the financial responsibilities that you once had, your mortgage is paid, and you still have most of your teeth! You'll hopefully be wiser, calmer and more patient, and you'll have life skills that will be useful in any

situation. You'll realise what really matters in life and understand how to cherish it.

18. Let go of old grudges, resentments and hurts if you possibly can. I know that it might be difficult at times, but holding onto them might actually be doing you harm mentally if not also physically. I understand that some of you may find it hard to forgive, but perhaps doing so can set you free to get on with your own life.

19. Be grateful. Dr Mark Rowe mentioned keeping a note of three things that went well in your day every day. This might sound almost too simple to be true, but focusing on the positive doesn't make the negative disappear; it simply helps you to reframe and to understand that there are still good things in life. I like the advice of the Vietnamese monk Thich Nhat Hanh to ask yourself, 'What's not wrong?' When you're giving out about the children making a mess, think about what's great about that – that they're having fun. When the dog has emptied your handbag all over the floor, ask, 'What's not wrong?' Maybe you'll find your keys!

20. Keep learning. And that doesn't just mean academically, although that's fantastic too. Keep an open and positive mindset and question things that you see and hear, particularly nowadays, when there are so many very rigid views on social media. Try not to

get sucked into them, but instead be curious about situations and people and be willing to give different views and perspectives a chance. You never know, you might learn something!